The Fact Book of Horse Breeds

The Fact Book of Horse Breeds

By Cynthia McFarland

© Stabenfeldt AS 2005
Text by Cynthia McFarland
All pictures © Bob Langrish, except
© Arnd Bronkhorst - page 8 and 163
© Gabrielle Boiselle - page 9, 32, 33, 73, 172 and 223
© Karin Tillisch - page 26, 49 and 56
© Marielle Andersson Gueye - page 154, 222 , 228 and 229.
© Ardina Strüwer - page 222.
Layout: Elsebeth Christensen
Published by Pony, 2007
Editor: Bobbie Chase
Printed in Italy
ISBN:1-933343-04-4

Contents:

PONIES AND SMALL HORSES...........133

HEAVY HORSES...........205

CONFORMATION...........235

Horses

Akhal-Teke

Background:
Recognized for at least 3,000 years, some say the Akhal-Teke is the world's oldest, purebred horse. In the Middle Ages, nomadic tribesmen from Turkmenistan in Central Asia cherished the hardy horses and treated them as part of the family. These horses thrived in the harsh desert environment, despite the scarce forage and extreme weather. In 1881, Turkmenistan became part of the Russian Empire and the horses continued to be bred in Russia. The breed's name refers to the Teke Turkmen tribe that lived near the Akhal oasis. Today, the Akhal-Teke is known as an excellent sport horse.

Conformation:
Small, refined head. Long, thin, high-set neck. High withers. Deep, narrow chest. Long back. Long, narrow frame with sleek, athletic build. Long, slender, muscular legs.

Characteristics:
Almond-shaped eyes. Shimmering, metallic gold polish over top the base coat, which can be bay, gray, black, dun, chestnut or gold. Flat, gliding gait.

© Arnd Bronkhurst - www.arnd.nl

What can I use it for?
Jumping, dressage and endurance racing.

How tall is it?
15 to 16.2 hands

Where does it come from?
Turkmenistan, Asia

Temperament:
Often known as a "one-rider" horse. Devoted, but can be obstinate if it doesn't want to do something.

8

Alter-Real

Background:
Portugal is the home of this noble horse which was bred to supply the royal stables. The name comes from the town of Alter de Chao and the word "real" means "royalty."
Andalusian bloodlines formed the breed's foundation stock in the mid-1700s. As a result of the Peninsular War of 1804 -1814, much of the breeding stock was scattered by the French and some of the best horses stolen. Later attempts were made to revive the breed by crossing Hanoverian, Norman, Arabian and English horses, but these influences did not succeed. Fortunately, Andalusian blood was reintroduced in the late 19th century and saved the Alter-Real. Once the Portuguese monarchy ended in the early 20th century, Dr. Ruy d'Andrade, a Portuguese equestrian authority, began breeding them, and in 1932, the Alter-Real stud was entrusted to the Ministry of Agriculture.

Conformation:
Attractive head with broad forehead. May have slight convex profile. Arched, well-muscled neck with high natural carriage. Wide, deep chest. Short back with sloping croup and low-set tail. Powerful hocks.

Characteristics:
Flashy action and high knee flexion. Ideal for high school "airs" or movements. Main colors are bay, brown, and gray.

© G. Boiselle

What can I use it for?
Classical equitation and dressage.

How tall is it?
15 to 16 hands

Where does it come from?
Portugal, Europe

Temperament:
Intelligent and spirited.

American Paint Horse

Background:
When Spanish explorer Cortez sailed to North America in the early 1500s, at least one of the horses he brought was a spotted sorrel and white horse. It is thought that this horse was the foundation for what became the American Paint Horse. Spotted horses were favored by various American Indian tribes, including the Commanches. The American Paint Horse was not officially named until the 1960s. The Paint has stock horse conformation similar to the American Quarter Horse. Paints come in a combination of white and virtually any other color and are found in three specific coat patterns: overo, tobiano, and tovero.

Conformation:
Attractive head with small ears and well-developed jaws. Well-balanced, athletic body with short back, deep, broad chest, and heavily muscled hindquarters. Strong legs.

Characteristics:
In the overo pattern, the dark color usually covers one or both flanks, and legs are usually white. In the tobiano, white usually doesn't cross the horse's back, and legs are usually dark. In the tovero pattern, one or both eyes are blue and the predominant color can be either white or dark.

What can I use it for?
Extremely versatile and athletic. Used for all types of Western and English disciplines and popular as a working ranch and cow horse.

How tall is it?
14 to 16 hands

Where does it come from?
United States, North America

Temperament:
Intelligent and easy-going. Hard-working and dependable.

American Quarter Horse

Background:

Known as "America's Horse," the American Quarter Horse was the first recognized breed native to the United States. In the 1700s, American colonists crossed imported English stallions and mares with the rugged little horses that descended from stock brought to North America by Spanish explorers. The result was a tough, reliable horse used for riding, working cows, pulling wagons and plows, and also for short races. Named for their great speed at the quarter-mile distance, the American Quarter Horse is considered by many as the world's most popular breed. They are well-known for their excellent temperament, versatile nature and remarkable ability at many disciplines.

Conformation:

Attractive head with small ears and well-developed jaws. Well-balanced, athletic body with short back, deep, broad chest, and heavily muscled hindquarters. May be compact and stocky, but some individuals are taller and more lean, thanks to Thoroughbred bloodlines.

Characteristics:

Versatile, hard-working, and dependable. Of 16 recognized colors, sorrel is the most common.

What can I use it for?

Used for all types of Western and English disciplines and quarter-mile sprint racing. Unequalled as a working ranch and cow horse.

How tall is it?

14 to over 16 hands

Where does it come from?

United States, North America

Temperament:

Gentle disposition, easy-going attitude and outstanding personality.

11

American Saddlebred

Background:
The history of this American breed stretches beyond the birth of the United States. In the 1600s, British colonists brought Irish Hobby horses and Scottish Galloways to North America. These two types were crossed to create a comfortable riding horse known as the "Narragansett Pacer." In the 1700s, imported Thoroughbreds were crossed with the Narragansett Pacer, resulting in a popular riding horse with the size and refinement of the Thoroughbred. This horse was known as the "American Horse," and in the 1800s breeders began referring to it as the American Saddlebred. In addition to Thoroughbreds, the breed was also crossed with Morgans, Hackneys and Standardbreds in the 1800s. Today's American Saddlebred continues its tradition as a smooth, comfortable riding horse.

Conformation:
Attractive head with small, neatly curved ears. Long neck with high head carriage. Short-coupled with round barrel and long legs. Naturally high tail carriage, but performance horses are often shown with "set" tails to enhance the way the tail is held.

Characteristics:
Animated, elegant and flashy. Known for its elevated hock and knee action at the trot. Famous for its smooth, single-foot gaits: the stepping pace and the rack. Predominant colors are chestnut, black, bay and gray. Palomino-colored and spotted Saddlebreds are popular.

What can I use it for?
Shown in both three-gaited and five-gaited classes. Popular for pleasure classes, both under saddle and in harness. Also used for Western pleasure, trail riding, dressage and jumping.

How tall is it?
15.2 to 16.2 hands

Where does it come from?
United States, North America

Temperament:
Personable and people-oriented. Curious and eager to please.

12

American Standardbred

Background:

The American Standardbred was developed in the late 1700s, from the English Thoroughbred stallion, Messenger. He was the great-grandsire of Hambletonian 10, which can be found in the pedigree of every Standardbred. The breed's name comes from the fact that horses had to trot a certain "standard" for the mile in order to be registered. American Standardbreds race at either the trot (diagonal gait) or the pace (legs on each side move forward and backward at the same time), and most races are one mile long. One of the most popular Standardbreds ever was Dan Patch, a pacer who covered a mile in just 1:55. The American Standardbred is recognized as the world's finest harness racing horse. When retired from racing, they can make good driving and riding horses.

Conformation:

Plain, but attractive head. Medium-sized neck. Deep girth. Long, powerful body.
Powerful, yet sleek hindquarters.
Croup usually higher than withers.
Strong, hard legs. Good hooves.

Characteristics:

Individuals tend to either trot or pace, but not both. Pacers are usually somewhat faster than trotters.

What can I use it for?
Harness racing, driving, general riding.

How tall is it?
15.2 to 16 hands

Where does it come from?
United States, North America

Temperament:
Kind and mild-mannered. Friendly and calm. Quick learner.

American Warmblood

Background:

The often confusing term "warmblood" refers to a type of horse that contains blood-lines from both "cold-blooded" horses (draft type) and "hot-blooded" light riding breeds, which are the Arabian and Thoroughbred. Numerous countries have their own type of warmblood, and Thoroughbred bloodlines are always a basic foundation. Developed to be the ideal sport horse, the warmblood typically excels at dressage, jumping and combined driving. The American Warmblood Society was founded in 1983 and represents sport horses of all bloodlines that have the conformation and physical ability that allow them to succeed in the classical disciplines.

Conformation:

Attractive head with expressive, large eyes and large nostrils. Long, muscular neck. Well-defined withers that slope gradually into back. Long, sloping shoulder. Overall rectangular body shape. Deep girth. Strongly-muscled back. Powerful, rounded croup.
Straight, strong legs with short cannon bones. Strong hooves.

Characteristics:

Known for its elastic gaits, energy, heart and athletic ability.

What can I use it for?

Excels at dressage, show jumping and eventing. Can be used for most English riding disciplines.

How tall is it?

15.2 to 16.3 hands

Where does it come from?

United States, North America

Temperament:

Even-tempered and obedient. Eager to please, calm and willing.

Anglo-Arab

Background:
Both the United Kingdom and France can take credit for developing the Anglo-Arab, which is a cross between the Thoroughbred and the Arabian. The speed and size of the Thoroughbred combined with the elegance and endurance of the Arabian make for a versatile and talented riding horse capable of competing at the highest international levels. Anglo-Arabs are known for their good temperament and athletic ability, and the breed excels at both jumping and dressage.

Conformation:
Refined head with both Arab and Thoroughbred characteristics and a typically straight profile. Long neck. Good, sloping shoulder. Deep chest. Short back. Long, slim, muscular legs with short cannon bones and well-made joints. Sturdy hooves.

Characteristics:
Known as an excellent competition horse.

What can I use it for?
Jumping, dressage, eventing, and most English disciplines.

How tall is it?
16 to 16.3 hands

Where does it come from?

United Kingdom/France, Europe

Temperament:
Intelligent, even-tempered and willing. Bold and honest.

Appaloosa

Background:

The colorful Appaloosa is a popular American breed, but horses with Appaloosa spots are recorded in Chinese art dating back to 500 B.C. Spotted horses were brought to North America by Spanish explorers in the 16th century. Some eventually escaped or were stolen. By the early 1700s, the Nez Perce Indians of the Northwest had obtained horses and carefully bred them to improve the stock. The Nez Perce were talented horsemen who used their spotted horses for hunting buffalo and as war ponies. When the Nez Perce were forced onto reservations in the 1870s, many of their horses were lost or killed. Fortunately, some survived and the breed didn't die out. The name Appaloosa comes from the Palouse River area of northern Idaho in the Northwestern United States where the Nez Perce lived. The phrase "a Palouse horse" later became "Appaloosa."

Conformation:

Ranges from compact and well-muscled to elegant and refined. Crossing with Arabians, Quarter Horses and Thoroughbreds can introduce some of the physical characteristics of these breeds.

Characteristics:

Durable and tough. Known for their colorful spotted coat patterns, which combine white with another solid color. Spots may be found over the entire body (leopard pattern), over the body and hips, over the back and hips, over the loin and hips, or just over the hips. Spots vary in size from small specks to three or four inches in diameter. Appaloosas typically have a white sclera, the part of the eye which encircles the iris. The skin is mottled or parti-colored. Hooves have boldly defined light and dark vertical stripes.

On occasion, an Appaloosa may be born solid-colored.

What can I use it for?

Very versatile. Used for many English and Western disciplines and racing.

How tall is it?

14 to over 16 hands

Where does it come from?

United States, North America

Temperament:

Friendly, gentle disposition. Good family horse.

16

Arabian

Background:

Search the background of the world's many horse breeds and you will find Arabian bloodlines. This ancient and revered breed was developed somewhere in the deserts of the Middle East as far back as 2500 B.C. Historians disagree as to the exact point of origin, but place it in the areas that are now Saudi Arabia, Syria, Iraq, Iran, Turkey and Egypt. To the Bedouin tribes, the Arabian was considered a gift from God, and the horse's courage, beauty and endurance was greatly celebrated. Bedouin tribesmen are credited with selectively breeding the Arabian, and many of today's Arabs trace back to this ancient desert breeding program. The Muslim conquests of the 7th and 8th centuries helped spread the Arabian horse throughout much of the known world at that time. The Arab's remarkable versatility and influence is recognized worldwide.

Conformation:

Refined, delicate head with wide, prominent forehead, large eyes and tapering, dished muzzle. High-set, arched neck. Pronounced withers. Deep, muscular chest. Long, sloping shoulder. Short, straight back with long, level croup. High tail carriage. Slender, muscular legs with well-defined tendons and broad, strong joints. Small, tough hooves.

Characteristics:

Excels at endurance riding. Arabs have 17 ribs, 5 lumbar vertebrae and 16 tailbones, while other breeds have 18 ribs, 6 lumbar vertebrae and 18 tailbones.

What can I use it for?

Extremely versatile. Used for riding and driving and virtually any English and Western discipline.

How tall is it?

14.2 to 15 hands

Where does it come from?

Arabian Peninsula, Asia

Temperament:

Spirited and willing. Intelligent and kind.

Australian Stock Horse

Background:

English Thoroughbreds and horses of Spanish stock arrived in Australia with the First Fleet in 1788. Additional Thoroughbreds, Arabians and Welsh Mountain Ponies arrived later, and all contributed to the development of the tough and versatile breed known today as the Australian Stock Horse. During World War I, the Australian Light Horse Regiments outshone most other mounted units, thanks to the amazing stamina of their horses. Known as the successor to the Waler, the Australian Stock Horse is a useful all-around horse with great endurance and conformation similar to the Thoroughbred.

Conformation:

Alert, attractive, Thoroughbred-type head. Sloping shoulder. Strong back. Deep girth. Powerful hindquarters. Long, graceful legs with large, flat joints. Good hooves.

Characteristics:

Known for its stamina. Comes in all colors.

What can I use it for?

Working cattle, endurance riding, and many English disciplines, including polo, dressage and show jumping.

How tall is it?

15 to 16.2 hands

Where does it come from?

New South Wales, Australia

Temperament:

Willing, even-tempered, courageous and intelligent.

Australian Warmblood

Background:
Beginning in the late 1960s, European warmblood stallions were imported to
Australia with the goal of crossing them with Australian mares, usually Thoroughbreds, to produce an Australian
Warmblood. Imported stallions included Holsteiner and Oldenburg bloodlines. The Australian Warmblood Horse
Association was founded in the early 1970s, and to be eligible, horses must have correct conformation and physical ability.
Australian Warmbloods have already successfully represented their home country at the Olympics.

Conformation:
Attractive head with expressive, large
eyes and large nostrils. Long, muscular neck. Well-defined withers that
slope gradually into back. Long,
sloping shoulder. Overall rectangular body shape. Deep girth.
Strongly-muscled back.
Powerful, rounded croup.
Straight, strong legs with short
cannon bones. Strong hooves.

Characteristics:
Strong, even cadence to gaits. Very athletic with
fine jumping ability.

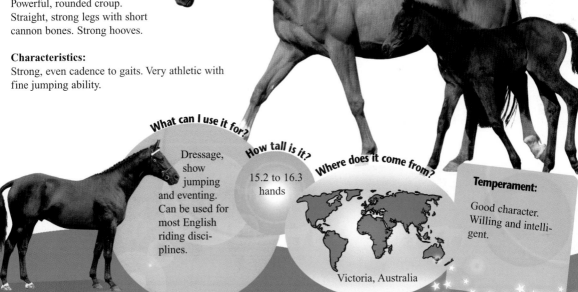

What can I use it for?
Dressage,
show
jumping
and eventing.
Can be used for
most English
riding disci-
plines.

How tall is it?
15.2 to 16.3
hands

Where does it come from?
Victoria, Australia

Temperament:
Good character.
Willing and intelli-
gent.

Azteca

Background:

After the Spanish Conquistadors came to North America in the 1500s, some of their horses eventually escaped or were turned loose in what is now Mexico. These horses were of Iberian descent and included the Andalusian. Herds of wild horses with Spanish bloodlines made their way across what is now the western United States where they were captured and bred by various Indian tribes. In Mexico, breeders later crossed the descendents of these horses with the American Quarter Horse to develop a versatile horse that is useful for rodeo events, working cattle, trail riding and competitive riding disciplines. Known as the National Horse of Mexico, the Azteca was recognized as an official breed in 1972.

Conformation:

Refined head with straight profile. Medium-length neck. Wide, well-muscled chest. Sloping shoulder. Short, straight back. Smoothly curved, well-muscled croup. Well-formed, straight legs. Strong hooves.

Characteristics:

Very versatile and agile. Good "cow sense," meaning they have a natural, inborn ability to work with cattle.

What can I use it for?

Rodeo events, pleasure riding, English and Western disciplines.

How tall is it?

14.1 to 15.3 hands

Where does it come from?

Mexico, North America

Temperament:

Docile, but lively. Obedient, inquisitive and even-tempered.

Barb

Background:

As one of the world's oldest breeds, the Barb has contributed to the development of many breeds, including the Andalusian and numerous others. Originally bred in North Africa many centuries ago, the Barb and its influence spread as a result of the Muslim conquests during the 7th and 8th centuries. Barbs were likely crossed with Arabians during this time. The Barb is fast and agile and known for its remarkable endurance. It can survive on scant rations and became a popular cavalry mount. The Barb is sometimes referred to as a Berber or Barbary Horse.

Conformation:

Head is usually long and has a straight or convex profile, narrow forehead and wide muzzle. Arched neck. Prominent withers. Upright shoulder. Short, strong back. Deep girth. Rounded hindquarters. Low-set tail. Slim, strong legs. Small, narrow, hard hooves.

Characteristics:

Extremely tough and known for its stamina. Easy keeper.

What can I use it for?

All-around riding.

How tall is it?

14.2 to 15.2 hands

Where does it come from?

North Africa

Temperament:

Energetic and alert. Can be unpredictable at times.

Bashkir Curly

Background:
This breed owes its great endurance and hardiness to the extremely harsh conditions of the Ural Mountains of Bashkiria, where it originated. Able to cover great distances and endure bitterly cold weather, the Bashkir is used for both riding and packing in its native country. The Bashkir Curly is renowned for its unusual curly winter coat, mane and tail. The curly coat sheds out in summer, and sometimes the mane also sheds, and then grows back in the fall. Foals are often born with crinkled hair coats and curly eyelashes.

Conformation:
Wide-set eyes. Sturdy, short neck. Flat withers. Wide body with deep girth. Flat, short back. Broad, rounded hindquarters. Straight, fairly short legs with strong, round cannon bones. Flat knees and strong hocks. Very strong hooves, usually dark in color.

Characteristics:
Main colors are rich chestnut, bay and light brown. Curly winter coat varies and ranges from tight, kinky curls to a wavy look. Thick mane and tail often form corkscrew curls.

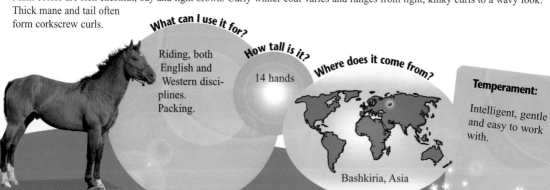

What can I use it for?
Riding, both English and Western disciplines. Packing.

How tall is it?
14 hands

Where does it come from?
Bashkiria, Asia

Temperament:
Intelligent, gentle and easy to work with.

Belgian Warmblood

Background:

In the 1950s, Belgian breeders crossed light-boned native farm horses with the stout Gelderlander to produce a heavy riding horse. More athletic Selle Francais and Hanoverian bloodlines were introduced in the 1960s. Dutch Warmblood, Thoroughbred and Anglo-Arab blood was also added to improve the size and speed. The resulting Belgian Warmblood has great athletic ability and an exceptional temperament. Belgian Warmbloods have been very successful in international shows and hold up well under the stress of competition.

Conformation:

Alert, appealing head, often with Anglo-Arab characteristics. Well-built, fairly short neck. Well-formed withers. Good, sloping shoulder. Compact body. Deep girth. Broad, muscular hindquarters and loins. Solid, correct legs. Sound hooves.

Characteristics:

Rhythmic gaits and great jumping ability.

What can I use it for?

Excels at show jumping and dressage. Can be used for most all English riding disciplines.

How tall is it?

15.2 to 16.2 hands

Where does it come from?

Belgium, Europe

Temperament:

Good-natured. Calm under stress.

Boer Horse

Background:
The Boer Horse, also known in its native country as the Boerperd, developed with the arrival of white settlers in the Cape of South Africa around the mid-1600s. Jan Van Riebeeck imported horses, including Persian Arabs, to cross with native South African ponies. Various breeds likely contributed to the Boerperd, including the Thoroughbred, Hackney, Norfolk Trotter, Cleveland Bay and Flemish stallions from the Netherlands. By the late 1700s, the Boer had developed a reputation as a multi-purpose breed known for its endurance and ability to work hard on a small amount of feed while still maintaining good condition. Their stamina as mounts during the Boer War brought the breed worldwide recognition as outstanding military horses.

Conformation:
Attractive head, typically with straight profile. High head carriage. Medium-length slender neck. Nicely sloped shoulder. Deep chest. Short, strong back. Well-muscled hindquarters. Slender, yet strong legs. Tough hooves. High-set tail.

Characteristics:
Intelligent, very strong and hardy. Known for its style and high action.

What can I use it for?
All-purpose riding and farm work, saddle seat, showing and fine harness driving.

How tall is it?
14.2 to 16 hands

Where does it come from?
South Africa

Temperament:
All-around good disposition and friendly personality.

Brumby

Background:
After the first horses arrived by ship in Australia in 1788, some of them eventually escaped or were turned loose and formed feral herds. In 1791, a soldier named James Brumby, who was also a farrier, came to New South Wales. Legend has it that when he moved to Tasmania in 1804, he left some horses behind, and when people asked who owned them, the locals answered, "They are Brumby's." Today the name Brumby applies to all of Australia's wild horses. Some Brumbies were crossed with Thoroughbred and Arabian stallions to provide cavalry mounts for Australia's Light Horse Regiments during World War I.

Conformation:
No consistent conformation traits, as Brumbies carry a variety of bloodlines, including draft, Thoroughbred and other light horse bloodlines. They are known to have exceptionally durable hooves.

Characteristics:
Strong survival instinct. Very hardy.

What can I use it for?
Stock horse.

How tall is it?
14 to 15 hands

Where does it come from?
Australia

Temperament:
Independent and intelligent.

Budyonny

Background:

In the early 1900s, Russian breeders created the Budyonny, also known as the Budonny. Marshal Budyonny, a hero of the Russian Revolution, helped develop the breed, which is named after him. The goal was to create a fine military mount by crossing the Russian Don with English Thoroughbreds. The Thoroughbred blood gives the Budyonny stamina and heart, making it a good competition horse for a variety of equestrian sports.

Conformation:

Intelligent, attractive refined head with Thoroughbred characteristics. Long neck. Solidly-built, well-muscled body. Deep girth. Rounded, muscular hindquarters. Long, slender, strong legs. Small hooves.

Characteristics:

Known for its staying power and good gaits.

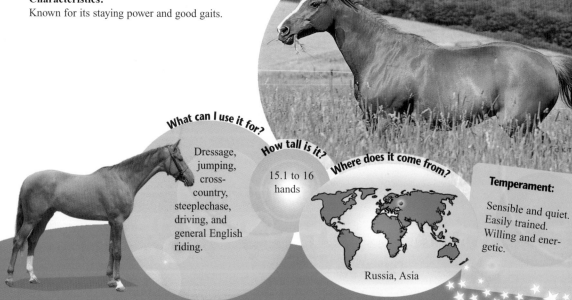

© K. Tillotse

What can I use it for?

Dressage, jumping, cross-country, steeplechase, driving, and general English riding.

How tall is it?

15.1 to 16 hands

Where does it come from?

Russia, Asia

Temperament:

Sensible and quiet. Easily trained. Willing and energetic.

Campolina

Background:
Iberian Horse stock brought to the Americas by the Conquistadors in the 1500s formed the foundation for breeds that would later be created. Around the 1870s, Cassiano Campolina, a breeder in Brazil, crossed a native Brazilian mare of Barb blood with an Andalusian stallion. The resulting colt became the foundation sire of the Campolina breed, named after Senor Campolina. Barb, Anglo-Norman, Andalusian, Holsteiner, American Saddlebred, and Mangalarga Marchador, another Brazilian breed, all contributed to the breed's development. Naturally gaited, the Campolina has a smooth four-beat "marcha" gait similar to a running walk.

Conformation:
Large aristocratic head with wide, straight forehead becoming convex just below the eyes. Well-set, arched neck. Powerful, compact body. Medium-length back. Rounded hindquarters. Sloping croup. Low-set tail. Clean, strong legs.

Characteristics:
Known for its comfortable, four-beat "marcha" gait which covers 6 to 8 miles an hour.

What can I use it for?
All-around pleasure riding and driving.

How tall is it?
14.3 to 16.2 hands

Where does it come from?
Brazil, South America

Temperament:
Gentle and kind. Good family horse.

Canadian Warmblood

Background:

The Canadian Warmblood Horse Breeders Association focuses on producing sport horses capable of competing successfully at the highest levels of equestrian sports. To be recognized as a Canadian Warmblood, horses must be approved according to conformation and performance. Canadian Warmbloods include horses of approved warmblood bloodlines, including Hanoverian, Trakehner, Oldenburg, Holsteiner, Dutch Warmblood, and Belgian Warmblood. Horses registered as Canadian Warmbloods have achieved international success in both show jumping and dressage.

Conformation:

Attractive head with expressive, large eyes and large nostrils. Long, muscular neck. Well-defined withers that slope gradually into back. Long, sloping shoulder. Overall rectangular body shape. Deep girth. Strongly-muscled back. Powerful, rounded croup.
Straight, strong legs with short cannon bones. Strong hooves.

Characteristics:

Known for its even, elastic gaits and fine jumping ability.

What can I use it for?

Excels at dressage, show jumping and eventing. Can be used for most English riding disciplines.

How tall is it?

15.2 to 17 hands

Where does it come from?

Canada, North America

Temperament:

Good-natured and obedient. Eager to please and willing.

Choctaw Horse

Background:
Named for the Native American Indian tribe, the Choctaw Horse is descended from stock originally brought to North America by Spanish explorers centuries ago. North African Barb, Garrano Pony, Sorraia, Spanish Jennet and Iberian bloodlines all contributed to the horses of the Conquistadors. Some of these horses strayed, formed feral herds, and were later captured, trained and raised by Choctaw Indian horsemen. By running them in isolated herds where they could not breed with other horses, they maintained a consistent horse of Spanish type with beautifully colored and varied coat patterns. In addition to solid colors, the Choctaw may be roan, buckskin, grulla, leopard, or pinto. A small herd of pure Choctaw Horses can still be found in Oklahoma.

Conformation:
Head shows Spanish influence, often with flat forehead and convex nose. Ears may curve inward. Well-crested neck. Narrow, but deep chest. Deep girth. Smooth-muscled, well-balanced body. Short back. Rounded hindquarters. Low-set tail. Short, strong legs, with short cannon bones. Thick-walled, sound hooves.

Characteristics:
Strong sense of self-preservation. Extremely hardy with great stamina. Some are naturally gaited with a comfortable, ambling walk.

What can I use it for?
Working cattle, trail and pleasure riding, all types of Western riding and sports.

How tall is it?
13.2 to 15 hands

Where does it come from?

United States, North America

Temperament:
Highly intelligent. Does not abide rough handling. Very loyal once bonded with owner.

29

Cleveland Bay

Background:
Britain's oldest horse breed, the Cleveland Bay descended from pack horses used in the Middle Ages. Used by traveling peddlers known as "chapmen," they were called Chapman horses and were bred to carry heavy loads over rough terrain. Later, Spanish Barb stallions were crossed with Chapman mares, and by the end of the 17th century, this crossbreeding had created a sturdy, yet attractive, pack and harness horse known as the Cleveland Bay. Crossing the Cleveland with the Thoroughbred resulted in an elegant carriage horse known as the Yorkshire Coach Horse. Today, there are two types of Cleveland Bay – the smaller type resembles the Chapman, while the taller type has the appearance of the Yorkshire Coach Horse.

Conformation:
Head often resembles the horse's Spanish-bred ancestors. Graceful neck. Sloping shoulder. Big-bodied with plenty of bone and substance. Deep girth. Clean, strong legs with short cannon bones and big joints. Hard, sound hooves.

Characteristics:
Body is always bay with black points on lower legs, muzzle and ear tips. Mane and tail are black. Very hardy and able to withstand harsh weather and tough going. Free, long stride. Great heart and stamina.

What can I use it for?
Combined driving, pleasure driving, cross country, hunter/show jumping, dressage and police work.

How tall is it?
16 to 16.2 hands

Where does it come from?
England, Europe

Temperament:
Sensible and highly intelligent with good temperament and strong character. Bold and honest. Can be spoiled if mishandled.

Colorado Ranger

Background:
Although named for the state of Colorado, the breed actually has its foundation in two horses from Constantinople – an Arabian and a Barb – which General Ulysses S. Grant received as gifts from Sultan Hamid of Turkey in 1878. Around 1900, these stallions were moved from Virginia to Nebraska where they were crossed with native mares belonging to General George Colby. Descendants of these horses were introduced to Colorado and proved themselves to be excellent ranch horses, often with colorful coats. In the early 1900s, Mike Roby of the Lazy J Bar Ranch in Colorado acquired two stallions, Patches #1 and Max #2, to use in his breeding program. The Colorado Ranger Horse, also known as the Rangerbred, was officially named in 1934. To be registered as a Colorado Ranger, horses must have either Patches or Max in their bloodlines.

Conformation:
Refined, attractive head. Compact and athletic build. Powerful hindquarters. Fairly short, strong legs. Sound, hard hooves.

Characteristics:
Great stamina and endurance. Typically has colorful coat patterns similar to Appaloosa, but some are solid-colored. May have Appaloosa characteristics of mottled skin and white sclera around eye. Rangerbred horses can be registered as Appaloosas, but not all Appaloosas can be registered as Rangerbreds unless they trace back to Max or Patches.

What can I use it for?
Ranch and cattle work, showing, performance events.

How tall is it?
15.2 hands

Where does it come from?
United States, North America

Temperament:
Versatile and agreeable. Excellent "cow sense."

31

Criollo

Background:
In the 1500s and 1600s, Spanish explorers brought horses of Andalusian and Barb bloodlines to South America. Some of these horses later escaped or were turned loose and large feral herds of horses ran wild. Later, the gauchos of Argentina carefully bred the descendants of those horses to create the Criollo, a tough, sound horse for working cattle. When the Criollo is crossed with the Thoroughbred, the resulting horse makes an excellent polo pony with both speed and endurance. The breed is known for its stamina, as demonstrated by Professor Tschiffely, an amateur rider from Switzerland who took two Criollo geldings and rode 10,000 miles from Buenos Aires to Washington, D.C. from 1925 to 1928.

Conformation:
Fairly short head with either straight or convex profile. Short, strong neck. Long shoulder and short, straight back. Stocky and sturdy build. Sloping croup. Well-muscled hindquarters. Somewhat short legs with short cannon bones. Small, hard hooves. Thick mane and tail.

Characteristics:
Known as one of the world's hardiest breeds. Comes in a variety of colors, often dun or roan. May have dorsal stripe down back and zebra striping on legs.

© G. Boiselle

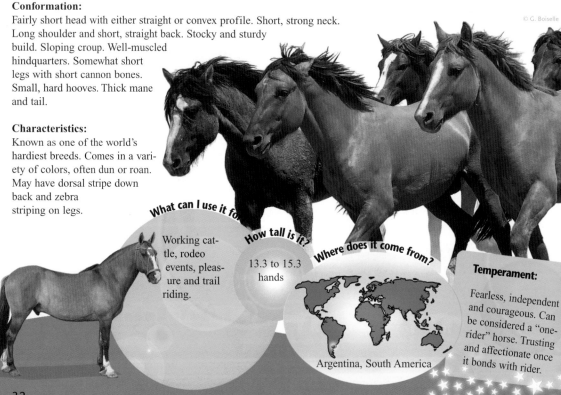

What can I use it for?
Working cattle, rodeo events, pleasure and trail riding.

How tall is it?
13.3 to 15.3 hands

Where does it come from?
Argentina, South America

Temperament:
Fearless, independent and courageous. Can be considered a "one-rider" horse. Trusting and affectionate once it bonds with rider.

Czech Warmblood

© G. Boiselle

Background:
A combination of European breeds contributed to the development of the Czechoslovakian Warmblood, which is bred in both the Czech Republic and Slovakia.
Nonius, Furioso, Thoroughbred, Gidran Arab and Shagya Arab bloodlines can be found in its heritage. Sturdy and reliable, the Czechoslovakian Warmblood is not known for its jumping talent, but it makes a good dressage horse and riding school mount.

Conformation:
Attractive head with straight profile. Arched, lean neck. Broad, low withers. Good sloping shoulder. Deep girth. Wide, deep chest. Long, broad back. Heavy, strong hindquarters. Straight croup. Well-made, strong, fairly short legs.

Characteristics:
Often chestnut, but can be any solid color.

What can I use it for?
School horse, dressage, and all-around riding.

How tall is it?
16 to 17 hands

Where does it come from?
Czech Republic/Slovakia, Europe

Temperament:
Obedient and easy to handle.

Danish Warmblood

Background:
Originally referred to as the Danish Sports Horse, this breed has been recognized only since the 1960s. Bred in Denmark, the Danish Warmblood was created by crossing Frederiksborg, Thoroughbred, Anglo-Norman, Selle Francais, Trakehner and Polish bloodlines. The result of these crosses was a versatile, well-made sport horse with talent, speed and boldness. The Danish Warmblood has many qualities that trace to the Thoroughbred, and is known for its soundness and strength.

Conformation:
Expressive head with straight profile and Thoroughbred appearance. Long neck. Nice, sloping shoulder. Prominent withers. Deep girth. Strong, muscular back. Powerful hindquarters. Long croup. Strong, well-made legs with short cannon bones and good substance. Well-formed, strong hooves.

Characteristics:
Athletic and versatile with good stamina.

What can I use it for?
Excels at dressage and cross-country. Can be used for most English riding disciplines.

How tall is it?
16.1 to 16.3 hands

Where does it come from?
Denmark, Europe

Temperament:
Agreeable, intelligent and courageous.

Don

Background:

This well-known Russian breed is named after the Don River area where it developed during the 18th and 19th centuries. Revered as the trustworthy mount of the feared Cossack warriors, the Don thrived in this harsh and unforgiving region. Later, the entire Russian army favored the Don, both as a mount and in harness. Karabakh, Arabian, Turkmene and Thoroughbred bloodlines all contributed to the Don, which became known as a distinct breed in the first part of the 19th century. The breed resembles a refined warmblood in appearance and is known for its hardiness, endurance, speed, agility and strength.

Conformation:

Attractive head with straight or slightly dished profile and wide forehead. High-set, lean, medium-length neck. Short, straight shoulder. Robust and wide-bodied. Muscular chest. Rounded croup. Sloping hindquarters. Low-set tail. Legs have well-defined joints. Back legs tend to be sickle-hocked. Hard, sound hooves.

Characteristics:

Known for its outstanding stamina.

What can I use it for?

English disciplines, pleasure riding and competition under saddle and in harness.

How tall is it?

15.1 to 16.2 hands

Where does it come from?

Russia, Asia

Temperament:

Pleasant and even-tempered.

Dutch Warmblood

Background:
Like other warmbloods, the Dutch Warmblood was developed by crossing a variety of breeds to create a sport horse capable of high level competition. German, English and French horses were crossed with native Dutch stock, and two other Dutch breeds – the Gelderlander and the Groningen – both contributed greatly to the development of the Dutch Warmblood. There are three categories of Dutch Warmblood: sport horse, harness horse and traditional Gelderland type, which performs equally well when driven or ridden. Breeding horses must meet strict performance and conformation standards.

Conformation:
Attractive head with straight profile. Arched, muscular neck. Prominent withers. Full, deep chest. Well-sloped shoulder. Straight, longish back. Greatly-muscled hindquarters. Broad, flat, short croup. High-set tail. Strong, well-made legs with long forearm.

Characteristics:
Excellent suspension at the trot.

What can I use it for?
Dressage, jumping, eventing, combined driving, and most English riding disciplines.

How tall is it?
16 to 17 hands

Where does it come from?
Netherlands, Europe

Temperament:
Intelligent and kind. Willing and eager.

Einsiedler

Background:

Horses were bred in Switzerland as early as AD 964, and the Einsiedler was developed around the 10th century using local breeding stock. In the 1800s and 1900s, the breed was improved with additions of Anglo-Norman, Holsteiner and Swedish blood. Also known as the Swiss Warmblood, the Einsiedler has been bred for equestrian sports and does well in jumping, dressage, cross-country and driving. Breed requirements are strict and horses are selected based on both conformation and performance.

Conformation:

Refined head with Thoroughbred characteristics. Medium to long neck. Long shoulder. Broad, deep chest. Medium-length back. Rounded, muscular hindquarters. Long, slim legs with substantial bone. Hard hooves.

Characteristics:

Usually bay or chestnut.

What can I use it for?

General riding and driving, jumping, dressage and cross-country.

How tall is it?

15.3 to 16.2 hands

Where does it come from?

Switzerland, Europe

Temperament:

Calm and honest. Willing to please.

English Thoroughbred

Background:
Some people mistakenly refer to any purebred horse as a "thoroughbred," but this is incorrect. The Thoroughbred is a true breed that traces back to 17th century England where it was developed from three founding stallions: the Byerly Turk, the Darley Arabian and the Godolphin Arabian. These three stallions were brought from the Mediterranean Middle East and crossed with native English racing stock. The resulting Thoroughbred could maintain its speed over extended distances, and forever changed the world of racing. The Thoroughbred is also an excellent competition horse in other equestrian sports, and its bloodlines have contributed to the creation of many breeds.

Conformation:
Refined, intelligent head with wide forehead and straight profile. Long neck. Long, sloping shoulder. Well-defined withers. Long body. Deep girth. Strong hindquarters and loins. Long, slender, yet muscular legs with clearly-defined tendons and flat joints. Powerfully-muscled hind legs.

Characteristics:
Extremely versatile with plenty of heart. Known for its speed at a distance.

What can I use it for?
Racing, steeple-chase, jumping, eventing, polo, hunting, showing and general riding.

How tall is it?
15.1 to 17 hands

Where does it come from?
England, Europe

Temperament:
Spirited and bold. Intelligent and willing.

Finnish Horse

Background:
The only breed native to Finland, the Finnish Horse has both European warmblood and draft horse bloodlines in its ancestry. Both draft and riding type Finnish Horses were developed. Today there are four types of Finnish Horses, also referred to as Finnhorses. These include a lightly built trotter, a draft type, a riding type, and a smaller pony type. Although not a big-framed horse, the Finnish Horse has notable pulling power, and is also very fast and agile.

Conformation:
Short head. Stocky neck. Upright shoulders. Deep chest. Long back with sloping croup. Strong hindquarters. Sturdy legs and hooves.

Characteristics:
Known for its longevity. Often chestnut with flaxen mane and tail.

What can I use it for?
Dressage, jumping, eventing, pleasure riding, driving, and trotting races.

How tall is it?
14.2 to 15.3 hands

Where does it come from?
Finland, Europe

Temperament:
Willing and even-tempered. Hard worker. Good family horse.

Florida Cracker Horse

Background:

In the early 1500s, Spanish explorers arrived in North America on the shores of what is now Florida. Among the horses brought on the journey were those of North African Barb, Garrano Pony, Sorraia, Spanish Jennet and Iberian bloodlines. Some of these horses strayed and formed feral herds. Indians and settlers later captured and trained these horses who had adapted to the challenging environment and become hardy, versatile mounts. They became popular with Florida cow hunters known as "crackers" because of the cracking sound of the whips they used to drive cattle. The Florida Cracker Horse took its name from this, as well.

Conformation:

Wide forehead, large eyes and well-formed nostrils. Sloping shoulder. Short back. Sloping croup. Low-set tail. Strong legs and tough hooves.

Characteristics:

Known for strength, endurance and cow sense. Some have a natural singlefoot or running walk gait.

What can I use it for?

Working cattle, trail and pleasure riding.

How tall is it?

13.2 to 15 hands

Where does it come from?

United States, North America

Temperament:

Dependable and easy to work with. Quick learner.

Frederiksborg

Background:
Originally bred as a mount for the military, this Danish breed was named after King Frederik II of Denmark, who founded the Royal Frederiksborg Stud in the 1560s. Horses of Spanish and Neapolitan heritage served as the foundation stock. The oldest breed in Denmark, the Frederiksborg was used to improve other breeds during the 17th, 18th and 19th centuries. They were known as fine riding horses with stylish, high action, and were also fashionable as carriage horses. Today, the Frederiksborg is considered a rare breed.

Conformation:
Head can have either a straight or convex profile. Medium-length, muscular neck with slight arch. Muscular shoulder. Low withers. Deep chest. Straight back. Broad, rounded croup. Long legs with strong, broad joints and clearly defined tendons. Fairly small, tough hooves.

Characteristics:
Always chestnut, often with flaxen mane and tail. Known for their elegant action.

What can I use it for?
Driving and riding.

How tall is it?
15.2 to 16 hands

Where does it come from?
Denmark, Europe

Temperament:
Pleasant-natured and easy to get along with.

41

Freiberg

Background:

Also known as the Freiberger or Franche-Montagne, this hardy breed was established in the late 1800s in the mountains of western Switzerland, near the French border. Mountain farmers liked the sure-footed and powerful Freiberg, and the breed was also very popular as a pack horse for the Swiss army. Norman, Anglo-Norman, Norfolk Roadster, Thoroughbred, Ardennais and Arabian bloodlines all contributed to the development of the Freiberg.

Conformation:

Small head with broad forehead and prominent jaw. Powerful build overall. Thick, wide, well-muscled hindquarters. Sturdy, strong legs. Good hooves.

Characteristics:

Sure-footed in the mountains. Known for its stamina and good nature.

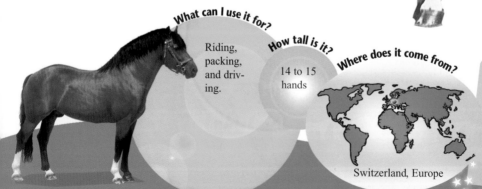

What can I use it for?

Riding, packing, and driving.

How tall is it?

14 to 15 hands

Where does it come from?

Switzerland, Europe

Temperament:

Easy-going, quiet and pleasant-natured.

French Trotter

Background:

Trotting races first took place in France in the early 1800s. To produce an excellent trotting horse, breeders in Normandy, France, crossed Normandy mares with Thoroughbred and Norfolk trotters. Some Standardbred blood was later added. The result was the French Trotter, a horse of stamina and substance that excels in racing at the trot, both in harness and under saddle.

Conformation:

Plain head with straight or aquiline profile. Prominent breastbone. Strong, fairly straight shoulder. Broad, well-balanced frame. Short back. Well-muscled, powerful hindquarters. Long, strong legs with substantial bone. Strong hooves.

Characteristics:

Known for stamina and its balanced, level trotting action.

What can I use it for?

Trotting races (both in harness and under saddle), driving and general riding.

How tall is it?

16.1 to 16.2 hands

Where does it come from?

France, Europe

Temperament:

Competitive and willing.

Friesian

Background:
The breed's earliest ancestors are believed to trace back to Equus robustus, a large primitive horse that lived during the ice age in what is now the Netherlands. In the 16th and 17th centuries, Andalusians were bred with descendants of this early horse. Breeders in the Netherlands province of Friesland developed the Friesian as a work horse. During the Middle Ages, Friesians traveled to other parts of Europe and knights used them as war horses. Today, the breed's stunning good looks, movement and personality make it popular as a dressage mount and for driving competitions.

Conformation:
There is the traditional "Baroque" Friesian and also a lighter-boned, sporthorse type.
The traditional Friesian is strong and heavy-boned. Fine, attractive head with small ears. High-set neck and high crest. Broad chest. Low-set tail.

Characteristics:
Jet black or dark brown in color with no white leg markings. Majestic, high-stepping action. Long, thick, wavy mane and tail. Feathers on fetlocks. Good mover. Well-suited for the collection required in dressage.

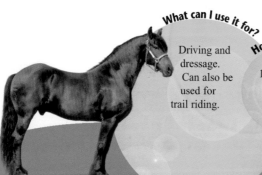

What can I use it for?
Driving and dressage. Can also be used for trail riding.

How tall is it?
15.2 to 16 hands

Where does it come from?
Netherlands, Europe

Temperament:
Quiet, easy-going disposition. Willing and kind. Good family horse.

Furioso

Background:
Hungary was the birthplace of this breed, which was established in the 19th century. The breed takes its name from the English Thoroughbred stallion Furioso, one of the foundation sires, along with another Thoroughbred, North Star. Nonius mares, another Hungarian breed, were crossed with Thoroughbreds to develop the Furioso breed. The result was a quality riding horse able to compete successfully in the major English riding disciplines, including steeplechasing and in harness. Furioso bloodlines also contributed to the creation of the Hungarian Warmblood.

Conformation:
Attractive, refined head with straight profile. Strong, graceful neck. Well-sloping shoulder. Medium to long back. Powerful hindquarters and loins. Strong, clean legs with well-formed joints.

Characteristics:
Typically bay, chestnut or black. Known for its endurance and soundness.

What can I use it for?
Riding and driving, all types of English disciplines.

How tall is it?
16 hands

Where does it come from?
Hungary, Europe

Temperament:
Intelligent, even-tempered and dependable.

45

Gelderlander

Background:

This breed takes it name from the prominent horse breeding province of Gelderland in its native country of the Netherlands. Originally used for light farm work, the Gelderlander was created by crossing several breeds, including the Friesian, Oldenburg, Anglo-Norman, Thoroughbred, Hackney and native horses. Hackney bloodlines gave the Gelderlander its stylish and elevated trot, making the breed in demand as a carriage horse. It is also popular as a riding horse known for its fine jumping abilities. Often chestnut, the Gerlderlander frequently has white markings on its face and legs, adding to its attractive appearance. The Gelderlander contributed to the development of the Dutch Warmblood.

Conformation:

Long head with straight profile and large, expressive eyes. Well-shaped, long, arched neck. Long shoulder. Prominent withers. Deep chest. Long, straight back. Short, flat croup. High-set tail. Muscular legs with strong joints. Large, strong hooves.

Characteristics:

Good jumping ability. High action at the trot.

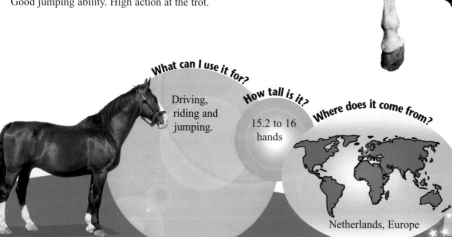

What can I use it for?

Driving, riding and jumping.

How tall is it?

15.2 to 16 hands

Where does it come from?

Netherlands, Europe

Temperament:

Kind and cooperative. Spirited, but gentle.

Groningen

Background:

This Dutch breed is named for the Groningen province of the Netherlands, where it originated. Breeders crossed Friesians and Oldenburgs with native Dutch stock to create a horse that could be used to work the heavy clay soil of the region. Suffolk Punch bloodlines were added to increase the strength and substance of the Groningen. In the 1900s, the Groningen was bred more as a carriage horse and riding horse. Only one purebred Groningen stallion could be found in the 1970s, but fortunately, the breed was saved. The Groningen contributed to the development of the Dutch Warmblood.

Conformation:

Long head with straight or convex profile and long ears. Short to medium-length muscular neck. Prominent withers. Broad, deep chest. Deep girth. Long back. Powerful, well-muscled hindquarters. High-set tail. Short, muscular legs with well-made joints. Good hooves.

Characteristics:

Usually black, bay or brown.

What can I use it for?
Driving and riding.

How tall is it?
15.3 to 16.1 hands

Where does it come from?
Netherlands, Europe

Temperament:
Calm, willing and easy-going.

47

Gypsy Vanner Horse

Background:
Colorful and people-loving, this breed has a long history in Europe. Shire, Clydesdale, Friesian, and Dales Pony bloodlines all contributed to creating the Gypsy Vanner Horse. Romany people known as Gypsies bred these hardy horses to pull their caravans or wagons. Living wherever they stopped that day, the horses had to survive on what forage could be found. Since they were literally part of the family, the horses also had to be docile and easy to get along with. Fortunately, these traits have been passed down through generations. Although they have been found in Europe for many years, the Gypsy Vanner Horse has only been a recognized breed in the United States since the mid-1990s, thanks to the efforts of Dennis and Cindy Thompson from Ocala, Florida.

Conformation:
Large, attractive, refined head with straight profile. Thick, muscular neck. Wide, deep chest. Short, broad back. Compact, muscular body. Strong, short legs. Abundant feathering on lower leg. Broad, tough hooves.

Characteristics:
Most common colors are piebald (black and white) and skewbald (brown and white). Abundant mane and tail.

What can I use it for?

Driving and riding in almost any discipline.

How tall is it?

12.2 to 15.2 hands

Where does it come from?

United Kingdom, Europe

Temperament:
People-oriented. Calm and gentle. Willing and kind. Good family horse.

Hackney

Background:

During the 18th and 19th centuries, this breed developed in Norfolk, England, from the bloodlines of the Norfolk Trotter, Thoroughbred and Arabian. The Hackney Stud Book Society was founded in England in 1883. Known for its elegant style and high action, the Hackney was extremely popular as a fancy driving horse before the invention of the automobile. The first of many Hackneys to be imported to America arrived in the 1870s. Many more came to America from 1890 and into the 1930s. Hackney Ponies have the same flashy, high-stepping action as the larger Hackney Horse and both are fashionable in the show ring today.

Conformation:

Small, attractive, alert head. Long graceful neck. Powerful shoulder. Broad chest. Compact body with level back and croup. Well-muscled hindquarters. High tail carriage. Medium-length legs with large, strong joints. Good sound hooves.

Characteristics:

Usually black, brown, bay or chestnut. Known for its spectacular high knee and hock action.

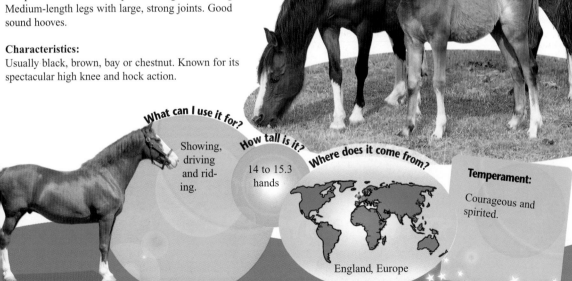

What can I use it for?
Showing, driving and riding.

How tall is it?
14 to 15.3 hands

Where does it come from?
England, Europe

Temperament:
Courageous and spirited.

Hanoverian

Background:
Developed in Germany, the Hanoverian is a warmblood known worldwide for its outstanding ability as a sport horse. The Hanoverian Studbook was officially founded in 1888, but this type of horse has been bred in northern Germany since the early 1700s. Holsteiner and Thoroughbred bloodlines were crossed with native mares, and some Trakehner blood was later added. Originally, Hanoverians were bred as carriage and military horses, but after World War II, they were bred primarily for performance. Hanoverians have been highly successfully in international competition and have won numerous Olympic medals in dressage and show jumping. Breed requirements are strict, and both sire and dam must be approved for their foal to be registered.

Conformation:
Refined, medium-sized head with large, expressive eyes. Long neck. Big, sloping shoulder. Pronounced withers. Medium-length back. Muscular hindquarters.
Well-made legs with substantial bone and large joints. Hard hooves.

Characteristics:
Known for its athletic ability and elegant, graceful gaits.

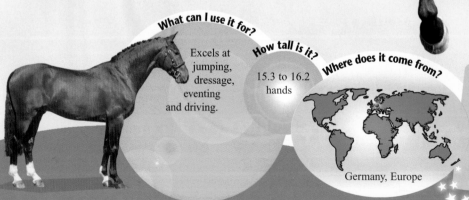

What can I use it for?
Excels at jumping, dressage, eventing and driving.

How tall is it?
15.3 to 16.2 hands

Where does it come from?
Germany, Europe

Temperament:
Sensible and even-tempered. Very trainable. Honest and bold.

50

Holsteiner

Background:

Considered the oldest German warmblood breed, the Holsteiner has been bred since at least the 13th century. Also referred to as the Holstein Horse, the breed is named after the Schleswig-Holstein area of Germany. Native German stock was crossed with Neapolitan, Spanish and oriental horses to create a horse known for its strength and dependability. Cleveland Bay and Thoroughbred stallions were later introduced to the bloodlines. Today, the Holsteiner is respected as a top performance horse in both jumping and driving at the highest levels of competition. The Holsteiner has also been used in the development of other warmblood breeds.

Conformation:

Attractive head, often with Thoroughbred characteristics. Kind, intelligent eyes. Long, arched neck. Good, sloping shoulders. Medium frame with strong back. Powerful hindquarters and loins. Strong legs with good bone and substance.

Characteristics:

Often bay. Known as an outstanding show jumper.

What can I use it for?

Excels at jumping, driving, eventing and dressage.

How tall is it?

16 to 17 hands

Where does it come from?

Germany, Europe

Temperament:

Willing and obedient. Level-headed and courageous..

51

Indian Half-bred

Background:
Developed in India around the start of the 20th century, the Indian Half-bred is a combination of breeds, as its name suggests. Primarily bred by the Indian Army, the breed was created by crossing oriental stock, Kathiawari, Australian Waler and English Thoroughbred bloodlines. Thoroughbreds managed to adjust well to India's climate and have proven excellent for crossbreeding. In addition to use by the cavalry, the Indian Half-bred also makes a good police mount and riding horse.

Conformation:
Straight profile. Ears may curve slightly inward at tips. Long, graceful neck. Upright shoulder. Overall wiry, light build. Sloping croup. Slender, hard legs with good bone. Tough hooves.

Characteristics:
Great endurance. Able to stand up to long hours of hard work.

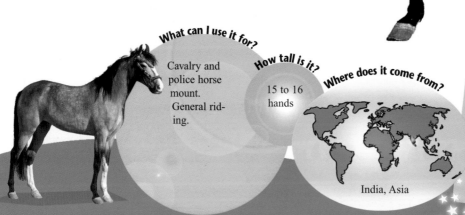

What can I use it for?
Cavalry and police horse mount. General riding.

How tall is it?
15 to 16 hands

Where does it come from?
India, Asia

Temperament:
Willing and calm.

Irish Draft

Background:
Also known as the Irish Draught, this breed originated in Ireland. Its ancestors likely trace back to the Flanders Horse of the Middle Ages. These heavier horses were later crossed with lighter breeds, such as the Andalusian, to create an all-around useful riding horse. An easy keeper, the Irish Draft is known for its hardiness, good disposition and natural jumping ability. When crossed with the Thoroughbred, the result is an outstanding and courageous performance horse.

Conformation:
Attractive head. Strong, arched neck. Good sloping shoulder. Powerful, deep body. Sloping croup. Strong, large legs with plenty of bone. Large, rounded hooves.

Characteristics:
Well known as a hunter.

What can I use it for?
Showing, hunter/jumper and cross country.

How tall is it?
15 to 17 hands

Where does it come from?
Ireland, Europe

Temperament:
Sensible, pleasant-natured and agreeable. Bold and willing.

Kabardin

Background:
Many horsemen consider the Kabardin the world's best mountain breed.
A native of Russia, the Kabardin has been bred in the rugged northern Caucasus since the 16th century. The bloodlines of Persian, Arabian, Turkmene and Karabakh horses can be found in the breed's heritage. Sure-footed in the most difficult terrain, the Kabardin thrives in high altitudes and extreme conditions. Used as cavalry mounts, they earned a reputation for outstanding endurance and the ability to negotiate steep mountain passes and river crossings. During the mid-1930s, riders on Kabardins covered an astounding 1,860 miles in 47 days over treacherous going. Today, crossing the Kabardin with the Thoroughbred is popular and results in a larger, faster horse.

Conformation:
Long head usually with a Roman nose. Narrow poll. Medium-length, well-muscled neck. Rather flat withers. Fairly straight shoulder. Muscular, short, straight back. Sloping hindquarters. Strong loins. Rounded croup. Hind legs are often sickle-shaped. Strong legs with well-defined tendons and good joints. Extremely hard hooves that never need shoes.

Characteristics:
Easy keeper. Usually dark bay, bay or black without white markings. Luxurious mane and tail.

What can I use it for?
Endurance riding, trekking in mountainous areas, packing and in harness.

How tall is it?
15 to 15.2 hands

Where does it come from?
Russia, Asia

Temperament:
Very calm and not easily upset. Reliable and obedient.

Karabair

Background:
Among the oldest breeds in all of Central Asia, the Karabair developed in Uzbekistan and Tajikistan. Arabian, Turkmene and Mongolian bloodlines can be found in the Karabair, which is used both for riding and in harness. There are three basic types within the breed: one for riding, one used for driving and a heavier type for packing. Known for its soundness, stamina and versatility, the Karabair is also used for racing in its native country. It was once popular as a cavalry mount.

Conformation:
Medium-sized head with either straight profile or Roman nose. High-set, medium-length neck. Prominent withers. Average shoulder without great slope. Wide chest. Wide, straight back. Long, wide hindquarters. Strong, fine legs with well-defined tendons. Hind legs may be cow-hocked.

Characteristics:
Good endurance for long rides.

What can I use it for?
Riding, driving and packing.

How tall is it?
15 to 15.3 hands

Where does it come from?
Uzbekistan/Tajikistan, Asia

Temperament:
Easy-going, but courageous.

Karabakh

Background:
Speedy and sure-footed, the Karabakh is named for the Karabakh mountain areas in Azerbaijan, where it has been bred for centuries. Native Azerbaijan stock was crossed with Arabian, Akhal-Teke, Persian and Turkemene horses to create the breed. Known for its speed, the Karabakh is popular for mounted games in its native country. Its coat is chestnut, bay or dun and is unusual for its shimmering, metallic sheen, which may be traced to the Akhal-Teke bloodlines in its heritage.

Conformation:
Small, refined head with straight profile. High-set, average-length neck. Deep chest. Average-length back. Compact body. Powerful hindquarters. Flat, wide loins. Wide, muscular croup. Low-set tail. Slender, long legs. Good, hard hooves.

Characteristics:
Good for mountain riding. Coat usually has a metallic gleam.

© K. Tillisch

What can I use it for?
Riding, trekking in mountainous areas and mounted games.

How tall is it?
14 to 14.2 hands

Where does it come from?
Azerbaijan, Asia

Temperament:
Easy-going and docile.

56

Kathiawari

Background:

Bred primarily in India's Kathiawar peninsula, this ancient breed takes its name from this coastal area. Held in high esteem by Indian households, the Kathiawari has a great amount of Arabian blood, which is obvious in its appearance. They were typically bred by elite Indian families, and were used as cavalry mounts during the 19th century. Kathiawaris are popular as police mounts and are often used for the native game of tent-pegging. Some Kathiawaris are born with a natural ability to pace.

Conformation:

Head has some refined Arabian characteristics. Ears curve inward and touch at tips. Medium-length neck. Wiry build. Strong, sloping shoulder. Short, sloping hindquarters. Low-set tail. Slender, hard legs. Tough hooves.

Characteristics:

Handles hot climates well. Known for its highly mobile ears which curve inward and touch at the tips.

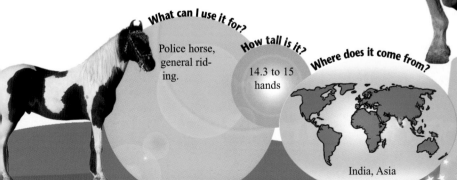

What can I use it for?
Police horse, general riding.

How tall is it?
14.3 to 15 hands

Where does it come from?
India, Asia

Temperament:
Agreeable, intelligent and friendly, but can be unpredictable.

Kiger Mustang

Background:
Like other mustangs, the Kiger Mustang descended from the Spanish bloodlines of horses brought to North and South America in the late 1400s and early 1500s. The unique fact about the Kiger Mustang is that they were isolated in a rugged mountainous area of Southeastern Oregon for years. This meant they did not cross-breed with other mustang herds or stray domestic horses. In fact, they were not discovered until 1977 during a roundup. Genetic testing proved the Kiger Mustang is directly linked to those early Spanish horses and is thought to be the best remaining example of the Spanish Mustang. In order to preserve this purity, the United States Bureau of Land Management maintains two special separate areas where the Kigers continue to roam wild in Oregon.

Conformation:
Clean-cut head may have slight convex profile. Prominent eyes, fine muzzle, finely pointed ears with slight hook at the tips. Medium-length neck. Deep, muscular chest. Short, broad back. Muscular hindquarters. Strong legs with dense bone. Small, tough black feet.

Characteristics:
Coloring is dun factor (dun, red dun, Grulla and claybank) and horses have primitive markings, such as a dorsal stripe and zebra stripes on legs. Manes and tails are often bi-colored with both black and lighter colored hair.

What can I use it for?
Trail and endurance riding, cattle work, packing, driving and all-around riding.

How tall is it?
13.2 to 15.2 hands

Where does it come from?
United States, North America

Temperament:
Curious and intelligent. Confident, bold and eager to learn.

Klepper

Background:
This Russian breed hails from Estonia, which was once part of the former Soviet Union. It is usually referred to as the Estonian Horse or Estonian Native, but was known as the Klepper in the past. An old native breed, the Estonian Horse looks much today as it did in the 14th and 15th centuries when it was used for working the land. It has been used for cross-breeding with other harness and saddle breeds, and has contributed to the development of some pony crosses, as well as the Torijskii, a breed just recognized in 1950.

Conformation:
Large, fairly coarse head with wide forehead and often with a Roman nose. Long neck. Wide, round chest. Low, wide withers. Long back. Average length, sloping croup. Short legs. Tough, but rather flat hooves.

Characteristics:
Easy keeper. Great endurance. Known for its longevity.

What can I use it for?
Light farm work and general riding.

How tall is it?
13.2 to 14 hands

Where does it come from?

Russia, Asia

Temperament:
Willing and easy-going. Energetic and good worker.

Knabstrup

Background:
Denmark is the home of this colorful breed, which descended from a spotted mare in the early 1800s. The breed takes its name from the Knabstrup estate of Judge Lunn, the breeder who is credited with developing these horses. Lunn crossed the spotted mare with a Frederiksborg and created a foundation line of spotted horses. Also known as Knabstrupers, their spotted coats come in a variety of colors and they are found in both pony and horse sizes. The Knabstrup has been popular as a circus horse.

Conformation:
Attractive, refined head. Strong, short, muscular neck. Muscular body. Broad, strong back and loins. Good legs with short cannon bones. Strong hooves.

Characteristics:
Spotted coloring is found on both body and legs. Hooves often have dark vertical stripes.

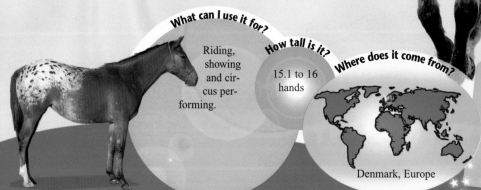

What can I use it for?
Riding, showing and circus performing.

How tall is it?
15.1 to 16 hands

Where does it come from?
Denmark, Europe

Temperament:
Intelligent and easy to train. Calm and well-mannered.

Latvian Draft

Background:
Beginning in the early 1900s, breeders in Latvia crossed native horses with western European breeds to create the Latvian Draft. Oldenburg, Hanoverian, Holsteiner, Norfolk Roadster, Ardennais and Friesian bloodlines all contributed to the breed's development, with the Oldenburg as the core. The Latvian Draft combines the best qualities of both work horse and riding horse, and is used both in harness and under saddle. The Latvian Draft can be found as a harness type and a sport horse type, with the sport horse type most popular today.

Conformation:
Large, but not unattractive head. Thick neck. Broad chest. Deep girth. Heavily-muscled, compact body with solid, well-proportioned build. Medium-length back. Powerful, rounded hindquarters. Hard legs with large, strong joints. Can be cow-hocked and may have short pasterns.

Characteristics:
Usually bay, brown or black.

What can I use it for?
Light draft and harness work, jumping, equestrian sports and all-around riding.

How tall is it?
15 to 16 hands

Where does it come from?
Latvia, Asia

Temperament:
Patient, willing worker.

61

Lipizzaner

Background:

The foundation for this elegant breed, also known as the Lipizzan, was created in 1580 when the Archduke Charles II established a breeding farm in Lipizza, also known as Lipica. Using Spanish stock, including the Andalusian and Barb, breeders crossed them with native white Karst horses, known for their high-stepping action. Arabian bloodlines were added in the 1800s. The Lipizzaner is forever linked with the respected Spanish Riding School of Vienna, where they were trained and excelled at the most difficult classical riding maneuvers. The first Lipizzaners imported to the United States arrived in 1937. They were saved from devastation during World War II by the heroic efforts of Colonel Alois Podhajsky of the Spanish Riding School and the American army under General Patton. Although slow maturing, the Lipizzaner is long-lived and often can work well into its 20s, and live into its 30s.

Conformation:

Intelligent head with Spanish influence may have slightly convex profile. Thick, muscular, arched neck. Overall compact, muscular build with substantial bone. Broad back. Powerful, rounded hindquarters. Strong, well-made legs with short cannon bones. Hard, well-formed hooves.

Characteristics:

Foals are born dark and turn gray as they age. Known for their soundness and natural ability to perform difficult riding maneuvers.

What can I use it for?

Classical equitation, dressage, driving, jumping and all-around riding.

How tall is it?

15 to 16 hands

Where does it come from?

Austria, Europe

Temperament:

Intelligent, sensible and calm. Bold and not easily intimidated.

Lokai

Background:

Developed in the 16th century, the Lokai is a mountain saddle horse bred by the Uzbek Lokai people in Tajikistan. A variety of bloodlines has influenced the Lokai, including Persian stock, Akhal-Teke, Karabair, Arabian, Tersk and Thoroughbred. Although among the smallest of the Central Asian breeds, the Lokai is versatile and known for its great endurance. It is not unusual for a Lokai to carry a rider as far as 50 miles in one day over mountain trails. In its native country, it is used for mountain riding, packing, racing and mounted games.

Conformation:

Plain head which may be coarse or bulky. Short to medium-length neck. Broad withers. Overall light, wiry build. Deep, broad chest. Straight, short back. Long, sloping croup. Legs are strong and solid, but hind legs can be cow-hocked. Tough hooves.

Characteristics:

Either gray, bay or chestnut. Good endurance for mountain riding.

What can I use it for?

All-around riding, packing and trekking in the mountains.

How tall is it?

14 to 14.2 hands

Where does it come from?

Tajikistan, Asia

Temperament:

Spirited and willing, yet sensible.

Lusitano

Background:

Related to the Andalusian, the Lusitano breed developed in Portugal, which is part of the Iberian Peninsula. Like the Andalusian, the Lusitano's heritage traces back many centuries to the revered Iberian Horse, which was used in battle long before the time of Christ. Lusitanos were used as cavalry horses, for farm work, classical riding and bullfighting. Known for its courage and high-stepping action, the Lusitano is famous as a bullfighting horse in its native country. The bull is not killed in the fight, but the horse must display great bravery and agility. The Lusitano's classic beauty and athleticism make it popular as a show and riding horse.

Conformation:

Well-made head with slightly convex profile, wide forehead and large, almond-shaped eyes. Thick, arched medium-length neck. Deep, broad chest. Well-defined withers. Strong, sloping shoulder. Short, strong back. Rounded, sloping croup. Powerful, muscular hindquarters. Low-set tail. Strong, slender legs with good joints. Hard hooves.

Characteristics:

Known for its power, grace and agility.

What can I use it for?

Dressage and classical English riding, pleasure and all-around riding.

How tall is it?

15 to 16 hands

Where does it come from?

Portugal, Europe

Temperament:

Calm, not easily upset. Intelligent, willing and honest.

Mangalarga Marchador

Background:

Many of the horses found in South America today still reveal the strong influence of the Spanish horses first brought to the continent by the Conquistadors centuries ago. The Mangalarga Marchador, known as the National Horse of Brazil, is no exception. An Alter-Real stallion was crossed with native mares of Spanish Jennet and Barb bloodlines, creating the foundation for the breed in the early 1820s. Brazilian land owners valued the Mangalarga for its smooth, comfortable ride and pleasant disposition. The breed has two special gaits, or "marchas." The "marcha picada" is a type of broken pace with little vertical movement, while the "marcha batida" is a four-beat gait in which the hind feet over reach the prints made by the front feet. Both gaits provide an exceptionally smooth ride. Mangalarga Marchadors can now be found in many countries outside Brazil.

Conformation:

Head has straight profile with rounded nose, typical of the Barb. Medium-length, well-arched neck. Medium-length back. Well-muscled hindquarters and loins. Legs have long forearm and gaskin, but short cannon bones.

Characteristics:

Known for its stamina and comfortable, smooth gaits.

What can I use it for?

Working cattle, cutting, jumping, polo, endurance, pleasure riding and showing.

How tall is it?

14.2 to 16 hands

Where does it come from?

Brazil, South America

Temperament:

Intelligent and attentive. Docile and easy to train.

Maremmana

Background:
Also known as the Maremma, this Italian breed originated in the Tuscany province of Maremma. There is some question about its ancestry, but most believe it was developed from Spanish, Barb and Arabian bloodlines, with the later addition of English blood through the Norfolk Roadster. The Maremmana was used as a cavalry and police horse, but is perhaps best known as the mount of choice for the "butteri," the Italian cowboy or herdsman. The Maremmana has a natural talent for working cattle and is steady and dependable under saddle.

Conformation:
Plain, but not unattractive head. Short neck. Somewhat upright shoulder. Fairly short back. Rounded hindquarters. Slender, but sturdy legs. Strong hocks. Tough hooves.

Characteristics:
Versatile and known as an easy keeper. Natural ability to work cattle.

What can I use it for?
Working cattle, mountain trekking and all-around riding.

How tall is it?
15.3 to 16.2 hands

Where does it come from?
Italy, Europe

Temperament:
Reliable, willing and pleasant-natured.

Marwari

Background:
Native to the Marwar region of India, the Marwari originated centuries ago in a harsh desert region. There may be Arabian, Turkmene, Mongolian and Kathiawari blood in its heritage. In addition to solid colors, the Marwari can also be piebald or skewbald. The Marwari descended from the war horses ridden by India's ruling families and warriors as early as the 12th century. Known for their exceptional hearing, the Marwaris are also said to have a keen homing instinct and have brought back riders who were lost in the desert.

Conformation:
Head with large, wide-set eyes and a tendency towards a Roman nose. Inwardly curving ears which form an arch when held forward. Arched neck. Deep girth. Rather upright shoulder. Wiry, muscular overall build. Muscular hindquarters. Hard, long legs. Tough, hard hooves that rarely need shoes.

Characteristics:
Handles heat well. Often born with a natural pacing gait called the "revaal."

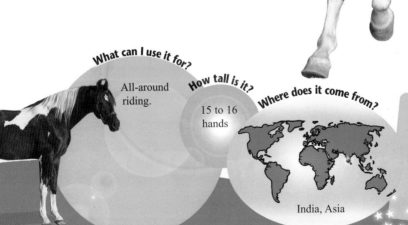

What can I use it for?
All-around riding.

How tall is it?
15 to 16 hands

Where does it come from?
India, Asia

Temperament:
Intelligent, proud and brave.

Missouri Fox Trotting

Background:
In the 19th century, settlers in the America's Ozark Mountains needed a reliable, sure-footed horse that could travel long distances in rough, mountainous terrain. They bred a versatile horse that could be used for riding, plowing, working cattle and pulling a buggy. The Missouri Fox Trotting Horse has Arabian, Morgan, Thoroughbred, Saddlebred, Tennessee Walking Horse and Standardbred ancestry. The horse's three natural gaits are its long-striding, flat-footed walk, smooth fox trot, and "rocking chair" canter. No special shoeing or training is needed to perform these gaits.

Conformation:
Graceful neck and well-shaped head with pointed ears, large eyes and a tapered muzzle. Deep chest. Short, strong back. Strong hooves.

Characteristics:
Very surefooted and comfortable to ride. Not a high-stepper, but its gliding gait is very smooth. In the Missouri Fox Trot gait, the horse is walking in front, but trotting behind as the hind feet have a sliding action. The horse's head nods in rhythmic motion with this four-beat gait, and the tail also moves with the beat. Head and tail carriage are slightly elevated.

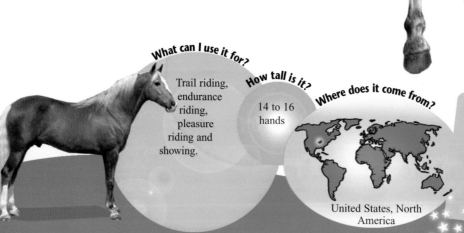

What can I use it for?
Trail riding, endurance riding, pleasure riding and showing.

How tall is it?
14 to 16 hands

Where does it come from?
United States, North America

Temperament:
Intelligent and gentle. Very trainable. Good family horse.

Morab

Background:

The best qualities of two separate breeds come together in the Morab, which was created by combining Arabian and Morgan breeding. Despite misunderstanding by some, the Morab is a distinct breed, not a half-Arab or a half-Morgan. American publisher William Randolph Hearst is credited with inventing the name "Morab." Hearst had a top Arabian breeding program in the 1920s, and also had Morgans, which he bred with his Arabians to create Morabs. The bloodlines of a registered Morab contain no more than 25% to 75% of either Morgan or Arabian.

Conformation:

Refined head with Arabian characteristics, such as dished face, large nostrils and eyes. Graceful neck. Deep chest. Compact, powerful body. High tail carriage. Strong legs. Tough hooves.

Characteristics:

Like the Arabian, the Morab holds the distinction of having 17 ribs, while other breeds have 18. Morabs also have five lumbar vertebra (other breeds have six), and 16 tail vertebra, while other breeds have 18.

What can I use it for?

Very versatile. Shown in harness and under saddle in many English and Western disciplines. Driving, carriage events, jumping, dressage, trail riding and ranch work.

How tall is it?

14.1 to 15.2 hands

Where does it come from?

United States, North America

Temperament:

Kind, yet spirited. Intelligent and willing.

Morgan

Background:
Considered the first American breed, the Morgan was named after Justin Morgan, a teacher, composer and horseman who moved to Vermont around 1788. He was owed money by a farmer who didn't have enough cash, so the man gave Justin Morgan two colts as payment. Morgan named the smaller of the two colts Figure. Although short in stature, Figure was stout and strong. He soon developed a reputation of being able to outpull, outwalk, outtrot and outrun other horses in New England. It is said that he was never beaten in a race, either in harness or under saddle. Figure also had the ability to pass on his stamina, beauty, strength and kind disposition to his foals. After his owner died, Figure was known by the man's name for the rest of his life. Morgan bloodlines contributed to the bloodlines of several American breeds, including the Standardbred, American Saddlebred, and the Tennessee Walking Horse.

Conformation:
Attractive head with straight profile, broad forehead, large eyes and short, alert ears. Powerful, compact body. Well-developed chest. Well-defined withers. Short back. Strong legs with short cannon bones. Hard hooves.

Characteristics:
Very versatile. Known for its soundness and power. Once considered the ideal mount for the United States Cavalry.

What can I use it for?
Combined driving, jumping, dressage, trail riding and virtually all English and Western disciplines.

How tall is it?
14.1 to 15.2 hands

Where does it come from?
United States, North America

Temperament:
Kind and loving disposition. Gentle, but with spirit. Willing and dependable.

Murgese

Background:
Developed in the 15th and 16 centuries, the Murgese is an Italian breed which originated from the Murge region of the country. Italian Draft, Neapolitan and oriental bloodlines were used to create the Murgese, which was once popular as a cavalry mount. The breed came close to dying out, but was revived in the 1920s. Used for light farm work, the Murgese is often crossed with warmbloods and Thoroughbreds to create a good riding horse. Murgese mares are also bred to male donkeys to create strong work mules.

Conformation:
Head has slight convex profile. Medium-length neck. Flat withers. Overall compact, light draft horse build. Upright shoulder. Medium-length back. Rounded, muscular hindquarters. Strong legs.

Characteristics:
Easy keeper. Short stride.

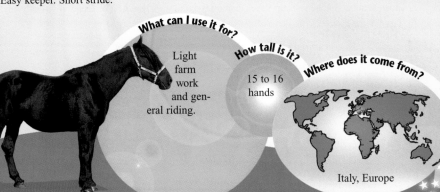

What can I use it for?
Light farm work and general riding.

How tall is it?
15 to 16 hands

Where does it come from?
Italy, Europe

Temperament:
Easy to handle and pleasant-natured. Energetic, willing worker.

Mustang

Background:

When Spanish explorers arrived in the New World in the early 1500s, they brought some of their finest horses. Some of these horses later strayed or were turned loose and formed herds. Through the centuries, other domesticated horses have joined these herds. Although some horsemen refer to any wild horse as a "mustang," the true mustang is a direct descendent of those Spanish horses. Some, such as the Kiger Mustang of southeastern Oregon, roamed in isolated areas where they did not crossbreed with other horses, and blood testing shows they trace directly back to the Spanish horses. Because their very lives depended on their hardiness and intelligence, only the toughest mustangs survived. This "survival of the fittest" made the Mustang unequalled for stamina in the mountains and plains of the American West. Some mustangs were used as cavalry mounts for the United States Army, and others became fine cow horses.

Conformation:

Head shows Spanish influence, often with flat forehead and convex nose. Ears may curve inward. Well-crested neck. Narrow, but deep chest. Deep girth. Smooth-muscled, well-balanced body. Short back. Rounded hindquarters. Low-set tail. Short, strong legs, with short cannon bones. Thick-walled, sound hooves.

Characteristics:

Strong sense of self-preservation. Great stamina. Some mustangs have a natural running walk gait. Can be found in virtually any color and coat pattern.

What can I use it for?

Working cattle, trail and pleasure riding, all types of Western riding and sports.

How tall is it?

13.2 to 15 hands

Where does it come from?

United States, North America

Temperament:

Highly intelligent and must be treated with respect. Very loyal once bonded with owner.

Nonius

Background:
Hungarian horse breeders developed the Nonius during the 1800s, naming it
after the foundation sire, Nonius Senior, who was foaled in 1810. This French-bred stallion was captured after Napoleon's
defeat and sent to stud in Hungary, where he bred many types of mares over the course of 17 years. Crossing with the
Thoroughbred yielded a powerful and sound all-around riding and harness horse. Nonius bloodlines also contributed to the
creation of the Hungarian Warmblood.

Conformation:
Appealing, yet somewhat rough-looking "ram's" head. Powerful neck. Well-proportioned, compactly-built body. Well-muscled hindquarters. Short, strong legs with plenty of bone. Hard, strong hooves.

Characteristics:
Smooth, free stride. Known for its longevity. Typically chestnut, black or bay.

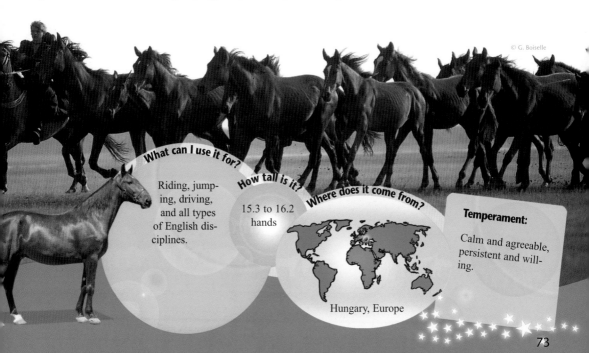

© G. Boiselle

What can I use it for?
Riding, jumping, driving, and all types of English disciplines.

How tall is it?
15.3 to 16.2 hands

Where does it come from?
Hungary, Europe

Temperament:
Calm and agreeable, persistent and willing.

Oldenburg

Background:

This European warmblood originated in the Oldenburg area of Germany and much credit for its development is given to Anton Gunther von Oldenburg. He founded the breed in the 1600s using Friesian, Spanish and Neapolitan bloodlines, with the goal of creating an elegant carriage horse. The Oldenburg, which is also referred to as the Oldenburger, was used primarily as a coach and driving horse at first. Over the next 300 years it evolved into a riding horse, thanks to the addition of English Thoroughbred, Anglo-Norman, Trakehner, Cleveland Bay, Anglo-Arab, Hanoverian, Holsteiner and Westphalian blood. Today, the Oldenburg is known in international competition as a fine jumping and dressage horse.

Conformation:

Noble, attractive head. Long neck. Long, sloping shoulder. Well-defined withers. Strong back with well-developed croup. Powerful, wide hindquarters. Well-muscled legs with sufficient bone and well-made joints. Nicely-formed hooves.

Characteristics:

Known for its long, energetic, rhythmic strides.

What can I use it for?

Dressage, hunter, show jumping and eventing.

How tall is it?

16.2 to 17.2 hands

Where does it come from?

Germany, Europe

Temperament:

Good character and even temperament. Takes well to training.

Orlov Trotter

Background:

Developed in Russia during the late 18th century, the Orlov Trotter was named after the man who created the breed, Count Alexis G. Orlov. Trotting races were popular at the time and Count Orlov hoped to breed a successful harness horse. He crossed Arabian, Danish, Thoroughbred, Norfolk Trotter and Mecklenburg bloodlines, and the Orlov Trotter's foundation sire, Bars I, was born in 1784. Continued careful breeding improved the breed, which was considered one of the world's finest trotting horses during the 19th century. The Orlov Trotter has also been used to upgrade other Russian breeds.

Conformation:

Small head with big, expressive eyes. Long, arched neck. Upright shoulder. Broad chest and deep girth. Muscular body with long, straight back. Powerful loins and hindquarters. Hard, strong legs with prominent joints and well-defined tendons.

Characteristics:

Gray is the most common color. Orlov Trotters sometimes race in traditional Russian troika harness with three horses abreast. The center horse trots while the two side horses canter.

What can I use it for?
Harness racing, driving and riding.

How tall is it?
15.2 to 17 hands

Where does it come from?
Russia, Asia

Temperament:
Bold and energetic.

Paso Fino

Background:

This naturally gaited breed originated from the Spanish Barb, Andalusian and gaited Spanish Jennets brought to the New World by Spanish explorers in the late 1400s and early 1500s. Settlers of the Caribbean islands and Latin America selectively bred horses to have a smooth, comfortable walk, and the Paso Fino flourished in Puerto Rico and Colombia. American servicemen stationed in Puerto Rico during World War II encountered the Paso Fino, and American breeders began importing the horses during the mid-1940s. In the 1960s, Paso Finos were also imported to the U.S. from Colombia. The Paso Fino has its unique gaits from birth and the name literally means "fine walk" in Spanish.

Conformation:

Refined head with straight profile. Large eyes, short alert ears. Medium-length neck with graceful arch. Fairly high head carriage. Sloping withers. Great heart depth. Strong back. Topline shorter than underline. Rounded hips and broad loins. Refined legs with short cannon bones.

Characteristics:

Known for its smooth, lateral, four-beat gaits: "paso fino" (slow and very collected), "paso corto" (moderate speed and collection), and "paso largo" (faster with moderate to full collection). The rider appears almost motionless at these gaits. The breed also walks and canters like other horses.

Paso Finos come in any color.

What can I use it for?
Showing, trail and pleasure riding.

How tall is it?
13 to 15.2 hands

Where does it come from?
Puerto Rico, North America and Colombia, South America

Temperament:
Spirited, but sensible and responsive. Friendly, people-oriented and willing to please.

Persano

Background:

Horses have been bred in Italy for centuries. This is the native home of the Persano, which was developed from Arabian, Thoroughbred, Sardinian and Salernitano bloodlines. The Persano's heritage makes it a riding and sport horse with plenty of stamina and courage. It is athletic and a good jumper.

Conformation:

Attractive head with expressive eyes. Elegant, arched neck. Long, straight back. Light, athletic build. Long legs with long cannon bones.

Characteristics:

Hardy and athletic riding and sport horse.

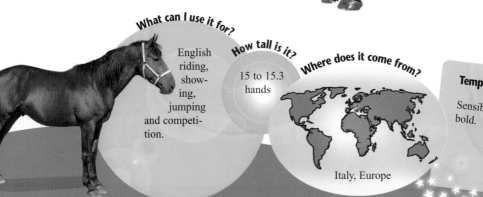

What can I use it for?

English riding, showing, jumping and competition.

How tall is it?

15 to 15.3 hands

Where does it come from?

Italy, Europe

Temperament:

Sensible, willing and bold.

Peruvian Paso

Background:

The Spanish breeds of Barb, Andalusian and Spanish Jennet contributed to the Peruvian Paso, which was developed in Peru by Spanish settlers. Although the breed has some of the same ancestors as the Paso Fino, which was developed in the Caribbean and Latin America, the Peruvian Paso is only from Peru. There, the breed was developed to carry riders around the plantation for many miles, often over rough terrain. They have stamina and great endurance, but are especially known for their smooth gait that does not bounce the rider at all. Some say the Peruvian Paso is the most comfortable horse to ride of all the world's breeds.

Conformation:

Medium-size head with straight or slightly concave profile. High head carriage. Arched, medium-length, well-muscled neck. Long shoulder. Short to medium-length back. Muscular, powerful body. Broad loins and sloping croup. Low-set tail. Short cannon bones.

Characteristics:

Known for its naturally-inherited four-beat gait that is somewhat similar to the running walk of the Tennessee Walking Horse. This smooth gait exhibits high action with the front legs, which swing outward, while the hind legs overstep the prints made by the front feet.

What can I use it for?

Trail and pleasure riding.

How tall is it?

14 to 15.2 hands

Where does it come from?

Peru, South America

Temperament:

Intelligent and spirited, but gentle. People-loving, very devoted, willing and energetic.

P.R.E. (Andalusian)

Background:

One of the most ancient breeds, the Andalusian is also known as the "Pura Raza Espanola," which means "pure bred Spanish." The Iberian Peninsula, part of which is now Spain, was the homeland of the Iberian Horse, which was hailed as the best war horse in the days of the Romans and Greeks. Named for the Andalucia region of Spain, the Andalusian traces it heritage to these courageous horses of old. Known for their elegant way of going, they are used for bull fighting and high level classical equitation. Andalusians have played a part in the development of many of the world's breeds.

Conformation:

Well-made head with slightly convex profile, wide forehead and large, almond-shaped eyes. Thick, arched, powerful neck. Deep, broad chest. Strong, sloping shoulder. Short, strong back. Rounded, sloping croup. Powerful, muscular hindquarters. Low-set tail. Strong, slender legs with good joints. Hard hooves.

Characteristics:

Known for its elegant, high, rounded action.

What can I use it for?

Dressage and classical English riding, pleasure and all-around riding.

How tall is it?

15 to 16 hands

Where does it come from?

Spain, Europe

Temperament:

Bold and spirited, yet gentle and easy-going.

Rocky Mountain Horse

Background:

Much credit for the development of the Rocky Mountain Horse goes to Sam Tuttle, who operated a riding stable at a state park in Kentucky. Among the trustworthy horses in Tuttle's barn was a stallion named Old Tobe, popular because of his comfortable ambling gait and genial disposition. When bred to a variety of mares, he passed on the unique gait, which is similar to a rack and can reach speeds of seven to 20 miles an hour. Many of today's Rocky Mountain Horses have the bloodlines of Old Tobe in their pedigrees. Blessed with endurance, they are very sure-footed and make excellent trail horses in rough terrain. The Rocky Mountain Horse likely has Spanish and Narragansett Pacer bloodlines as its foundation stock.

Conformation:

Attractive, finely-made head. Medium build. Nice sloping shoulder. Wide chest. Slender, but strong legs. Sturdy hooves.

Characteristics:

Always solid-colored. Often a "chocolate" chestnut color with flaxen mane and tail. Known for their four-beat ambling gait.

What can I use it for?

Trail and pleasure riding, showing and working cattle.

How tall is it?

14 to 16 hands

Where does it come from?

United States, North America

Temperament:

Calm and easy-going. Gentle and pleasant-natured.

Russian Riding Horse

Background:
A variety of bloodlines, including Arabian, Persian, Spanish, Neopolitan, Danish and English Thoroughbred, were all combined to create the Russian Riding Horse. The breed's original name was Orlov-Rostopchin and dates back to the 1840s when the horses were bred for dressage, as well as carriage and military use. Typically black in color, the Russian Riding Horse is known for its athleticism and beauty. They have proven to be fine competitors in the sports of jumping, dressage, and eventing, where their courage and physical ability are put to the test. It is also known as the Russian Saddle Horse.

Conformation:
Attractive head. Long, graceful neck with high carriage. Compact, yet refined body type. Long legs with good bone and well-made joints.

Characteristics:
Very athletic. Body is well-suited for collection and extension.

What can I use it for?
Dressage, eventing, jumping, working hunter and general riding.

How tall is it?
15.1 to 17.1 hands

Where does it come from?
Russia, Asia

Temperament:
Willing and highly trainable. Sensitive, but not flighty.

Russian Trotter

Background:

Trotting races have long been popular in Russia. By the turn of the 20th century, imported Standardbreds from America had proven themselves faster at harness racing than Russia's native Orlov Trotter. For improved speed and conformation, Russian breeders began crossing the American Standardbred with the Orlov Trotter, and the result was the Russian Trotter. Additional crossbreeding with American Standardbreds still continues to some degree. In its native country, the Russian Trotter must meet strict breed requirements for conformation and must also pass performance tests on the racetrack. The Russian Trotter is usually faster than the Orlov Trotter.

Conformation:

Plain, light head with straight profile and wide forehead. Long, straight neck. Medium height withers. Light overall build. Straight, well-muscled back and loins. Flat, broad croup. Long legs with well-developed muscles and tendons. Sound, hard hooves.

Characteristics:

Appearance is similar to the American Standardbred.

What can I use it for?
Harness racing and driving.

How tall is it?
15.3 to 16.3 hands

Where does it come from?
Russia, Asia.

Temperament:
Bold and competitive, but not usually high-strung.

Salernitano

Background:

Also known as the Salerno, this Italian breed was developed during the 16th century in the Salerno area, not far from Naples. The Salernitano was created from the bloodlines of Andalusians, Barbs, Arabians and Spanish stock. Once popular as a mount for the Italian Army, the Salernitano is now used for general riding and equestrian competitions. Recognized for their athleticism and jumping ability, the breed makes a fine sport horse, and has been used to upgrade regional Italian riding horses.

Conformation:

Large refined head with straight profile and square forehead. Long muscular neck. Prominent withers. Good shoulder. Well-proportioned back with short loins. Strong sloping hindquarters. Muscular croup. Well-formed legs with good bone.

Characteristics:

Adapts well to hot climates. Excellent jumper.

What can I use it for?

English riding disciplines and sport, jumping and competition.

How tall is it?

16 to 17 hands

Where does it come from?

Italy, Europe

Temperament:

Intelligent and responsive. Spirited and energetic, but kind.

83

San Fratellano

Background:
This old Italian breed was developed from 200 mares of Normandy blood that were brought to Sicily around the year 1,000. Arabian and possibly some other bloodlines were crossed on these mares to create a horse that could be used for both farm work and riding. The San Fratellano is known for its energy and hardiness.

Conformation:
Head can have either a straight or convex profile. Overall fine-boned build. Short, upright, shoulder. Long back. Strong legs. Good, hard hooves.

Characteristics:
Usually bay or black with no white markings.

What can I use it for?
Riding and farm work.

How tall is it?
14.3 to 15.3 hands

Where does it come from?
Italy, Europe

Temperament:
Friendly, but spirited. Sensible and energetic.

Sardinian

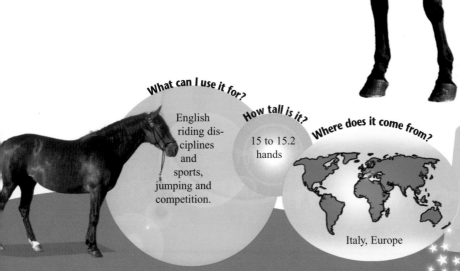

Background:
Horses have been bred on the Italian island of Sardinia for centuries. Named for its native land, the Sardinian developed in the 15th century from a foundation of Barb, Arabian and Thoroughbred bloodlines. Their heritage gives the breed an oriental appearance. Sardinians are known as hardy riding horses with great stamina, and their jumping ability is exceptional, which makes them good competition horses.

Conformation:
Somewhat plain, but not unattractive head. Elegant, arched neck. Long straight back.
Light overall build that resembles an Anglo-Arab. Long legs with long cannon bones.

Characteristics:
Usually bay or brown. Excellent jumper.

What can I use it for?
English riding disciplines and sports, jumping and competition.

How tall is it?
15 to 15.2 hands

Where does it come from?
Italy, Europe

Temperament:
Bold and courageous. Intelligent and willing.

Sella Italiano

Background:

This Italian breed is a useful cross between earlier, heavy horses bred for work and the lighter, faster Arabian, Thoroughbred, and Anglo-Arab. Italian breeders wanted to develop a riding horse with reliability and a good work ethic, but one that also had elegance and stamina. The resulting Sella Italiano is both fast and responsive, and is used for a variety of equestrian sports, including jumping and dressage.

Conformation:

Elegant, proportionate head. Long, well-made neck. Good shoulder. Strong, medium-length back. Muscular hindquarters. Sloping croup. Long, slender legs.

Characteristics:

Very athletic and bred for sport.

What can I use it for?
Jumping, dressage, endurance riding and all-around riding.

How tall is it?
15 to 16.3 hands

Where does it come from?

Italy, Europe

Temperament:
Lively and bold, but reliable.

Selle Francais

Background:

A warmblood, the Selle Francais is a unique mix of breeds. During the 19th century, breeders in Normandy, France, bred imported English Thoroughbreds with their native Normandy mares. In addition to Thoroughbred blood, Arabians, Anglo-Arabs, French Trotters and even the Norman war horse all contributed to the resulting Anglo-Norman, which produced both a saddle horse and a draft type. The saddle type Anglo-Norman became the most recognized foundation stock of today's Selle Francais. After World War II, French breeders concentrated on developing a riding horse with stamina, athletic ability and speed. In 1958, this breed was officially named the Selle Francais and is known for its galloping and jumping ability.

Conformation:

Fine, expressive head. Long neck. Strong back. Powerful hindquarters. Sturdy legs with substantial bone. Large hooves.

Characteristics:

Not as large or heavy as some warmblood breeds. Resembles a big-boned Thoroughbred with strong, elegant body type.

What can I use it for?

Excels at jumping and eventing. Also used for dressage and hunting.

How tall is it?

15.3 to 16.3 hands

Where does it come from?

France, Europe

Temperament:

Calm and sensible, but not overly sensitive. Intelligent, kind and forgiving. Very people-oriented.

Shagya Arab

Background:

The Babolna Stud in Hungary is the home of this special Arabian breed, which was developed in the 1800s. The Shagya Arab is a result of crossing desert-bred Arabians with native Babolna stock. The breed is named for its foundation sire, Shagya, who was born in 1830. Shagya Arabs have many of the same bloodlines as the desert-bred Arabian which originated with the Bedouins, but they are generally taller and more robust. They have the Arabian's classic type, endurance and versatility, and they excel under saddle and in harness. Once used as cavalry mounts, today their excellent gaits and jumping ability make them desirable as competition horses.

Conformation:

Refined head with wide, prominent forehead, large eyes and dished muzzle. High-set, arched neck. Pronounced withers. Deep, muscular chest. Compact, robust body. Long, sloping shoulder. Short, straight back with long, level croup. High tail carriage. Slender, muscular legs with plenty of bone and broad, strong joints. Tough hooves.

Characteristics:

Taller with a bigger frame and more substance than most desert-bred Arabs.

What can I use it for?
Dressage, jumping, eventing, hunting, driving, and all-around riding.

How tall is it?
15 to 15.2 hands

Where does it come from?
Hungary, Europe

Temperament:
Pleasant-natured. Intelligent and willing.

Shales Horse

Background:
Directly descended from the Norfolk Trotter, the Shales Horse hails from
England and traces back to the famous Darley Arabian. The horse takes its
name from the Shales family of Norfolk, which was highly respected as a
breeder of fine trotting horses.

Today, the modern Shales Horse has been bred since the early 1920s by the
Colquhoun family, and is recognized for its versatility both in harness
and under saddle. Known as a good cross to produce athletic performance horses, the Shales Horse also contributed to the development of the Hackney breed.

Conformation:
Intelligent, attractive head with expressive eyes. Slightly
arched, medium-length neck. Sloping shoulder. Deep
chest. Long back. Long sloping, well-muscled
hindquarters. Strong, clean legs with well-defined
joints and good bone.

Characteristics:
Very versatile and hardy.

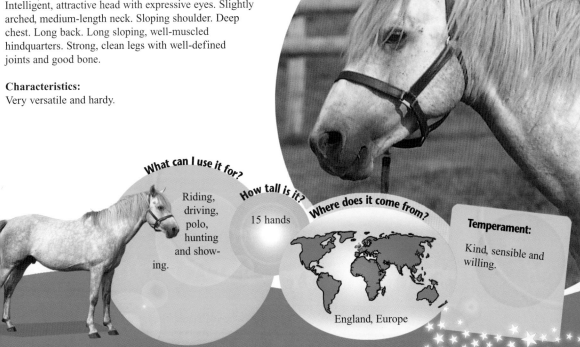

What can I use it for?

Riding, driving, polo, hunting and show-ing.

How tall is it?

15 hands

Where does it come from?

England, Europe

Temperament:

Kind, sensible and willing.

Spotted Saddle Horse

Background:

Spanish explorers brought the early ancestors of the Spotted Saddle Horse to North America, and a number of these horses later escaped. Some of these mounts were spotted and naturally gaited. Breeders selected gaited horses to cross with spotted horses to produce a colorful, smooth-riding horse that was named the Spotted Saddle Horse. The breed is known for its long-reaching show walk, "show gait" and rocking-chair canter. In the "show gait," which is unique to the breed, the horse's feet each hit the ground separately at regular intervals. This is an extremely smooth, quick gait in which the horse moves at 10 to 20 miles-per-hour.

Conformation:

Chiseled, attractive head that is carried high. Medium to long neck. Short to medium-length back. Long sloping shoulder and hip. Legs set squarely under the body. Tough hooves.

Characteristics:

Known for the show walk, "show gait," and rocking-chair canter. Widely varying patterns and color combinations.

What can I use it for?

Trail, pleasure riding and showing.

How tall is it?

14.3 to 16 hands

Where does it come from?

United States, North America

Temperament:

Docile and easy-going. People-oriented and eager to please.

Swedish Warmblood

Background:
One of the world's oldest warmblood breeds, the Swedish Warmblood is the result of careful breeding over the years. Horses have been bred in Flyinge, Sweden, since the 12th century. The Swedish Warmblood is a result of crossing native horses with the Friesian, Thoroughbred, Anglo-Norman, Hanoverian and Trakehner. Most warmblood breeds were initially bred as carriage and work horses, but the Swedish Warmblood was intended as a riding horse from the start. Athletic and versatile, the breed has excelled in the highest levels of international competition, particularly in dressage and combined driving. The Swedish breeding program is rigid, and both mares and stallions must be approved.

Conformation:
Handsome head with wide forehead and alert expression. Long neck. Strong shoulder that may be rather straight. Deep girth. Compact, well-muscled body. Straight back. Powerful, rounded hindquarters. Strong legs with short cannon bones.

Characteristics:
Known for its elegant gaits, jumping ability and positive attitude.

What can I use it for?
Dressage, jumping, combined driving, and most English riding disciplines.

How tall is it?
15 to 17 hands

Where does it come from?
Sweden, Europe

Temperament:
Intelligent and takes well to training. Kind, willing and bold.

Tennessee Walking Horse

Background:
Recognized as an official breed in 1947, the Tennessee Walking Horse bears the name of its home state. Breeders wanted a horse that was comfortable for hours of riding, but still would be stylish. The Narragansett Pacer, Thoroughbred, Morgan, Standardbred and American Saddlebred all contributed to the formation of the Tennessee Walker. Popular in the show ring and for pleasure riding, the breed is known for three distinct gaits: the flat walk, running walk, and "rocking chair" canter. The flat walk covers four to eight miles an hour, while the unique running walk is an extremely smooth gait that can reach speeds of 10 to 20 miles per hour. Tennessee Walking Horses come in many different colors, including colorful pinto markings.

Conformation:
Fairly plain head with straight profile and small ears. Long sloping shoulder and hip.
Short back. Strong, short-coupled body.
Conformation allows horse to have a long stride.

Characteristics:
The breed is famous for its running walk, a smooth, gliding four-beat walk during which the hind legs reach well underneath the body and over stride the prints made by the front feet. When the horse is walking, its head nods in rhythm, the ears flop back and forth, and sometimes the teeth also snap to the tempo of the walk.

What can I use it for?
Pleasure and trail riding. Showing in both English and Western disciplines.

How tall is it?
15 to 17 hands

Where does it come from?
United States, North America

Temperament:
Gentle and docile. People-oriented, forgiving and willing to please.

Trakehner

Background:
One of the oldest European warmblood breeds, the Trakehner was bred for centuries in what was once East Prussia. The correct full name is actually "the East Prussian Warmblood Horse of Trakehner Origin." English Thoroughbreds and Arabians were crossed with local East Prussian horses to create the Trakehner. They proved to have great endurance and comfortable gaits, and were used as military mounts and performance horses and even for light draft work. To avoid capture during World War II, Trakehners were relocated to West Germany where breeding continued after 1945. Breed requirements are strict and stallions must be tested and approved. Highly successful in international competition, the Trakehner has been used to upgrade other European breeds.

Conformation:
Refined head with broad forehead and large, wide-set eyes. Long, graceful neck. Deep, sloping shoulder. Large, solid body with rectangular frame. Deep girth. Medium-length back. Powerful hindquarters. Long, sloping croup. Good, straight legs with short cannon bones. Sound hooves.

Characteristics:
Slow maturing. Known for its graceful, ground-covering trot.

What can I use it for?
Excels at dressage and jumping.

How tall is it?
15.1 to 16.2 hands

Where does it come from?
Germany, Europe

Temperament:
Intelligent and kind. Quick learner, patient and accepting.

Ukrainian Riding Horse

Background:
One of 45 horse breeds raised in Russia, the Ukrainian Riding Horse was developed in the Ukraine around the end of World War II. The breed was created using the bloodlines of the Hanoverian, Trakehner, Nonius, Furioso and Thoroughbred. Used as an all-around riding and equestrian sport horse, the Ukrainian Riding Horse is among the top five most popular Russian breeds for riding sports. They are capable of competing successfully at international levels and are used for both riding and driving.

Conformation:
Attractive head with wide forehead. Long, elegant neck. Good sloping shoulder. Deep girth. Medium-length back. Well-muscled hindquarters. Well-made legs with strong joints and good bone.

Characteristics:
Typically bay, black or chestnut. Very athletic.

What can I use it for?
English riding disciplines and sports, including dressage and driving.

How tall is it?
15.1 to 16.1 hands

Where does it come from?
Russia, Asia

Temperament:
Spirited, yet sensible.

Waler

Background:
Named for the colony of New South Wales, the Waler has a mixed ancestry. It was developed from stock brought to Australia by settlers in the late 1700s. Bloodlines of Spanish, Arabian, Barb, Dutch stock and English Thoroughbred all contributed to the Waler's heritage. The resulting horse was agile, fast and tough, all necessary qualities for Australia's vast, untamed land. Walers proved to be exceptional cavalry mounts with outstanding stamina and heart. Known for their hardiness, they also developed a good reputation on the country's large cattle stations. In the mid-1900s, the Waler evolved into the Australian Stock Horse.

Conformation:
Attractive, intelligent head with broad forehead and large nostrils. Medium to long neck. Sloping shoulder. Well-defined withers that are higher than the croup. Deep chest. Strong, medium-length back. Powerful, rounded hindquarters. Well-developed, strong legs with good joints. Hard hooves.

Characteristics:
Known for soundness and versatility.

What can I use it for?
Working cattle, rodeo, polo, dressage, jumping, eventing, trail and general riding.

How tall is it?
15 to 16 hands

Where does it come from?
New South Wales, Australia

Temperament:
Intelligent, obedient, willing and quiet.

Westphalian

Background:
As with other German warmblood breeds, the Westphalian is named for the region of Germany from which it originated, in this case, Westphalia. The breed registry opened in 1904, and in the early days, the breed was founded with Oldenburg and Anglo-Norman stock. Since the 1920s, however, the Westphalian breeding program has been based on Hanoverian bloodlines, with some Trakehner and Thoroughbred blood added. Westphalians have been used as military mounts and have also excelled as show jumpers and in dressage competition. They make fine driving horses, as well.

Conformation:
Noble, medium-sized head with large, expressive eyes. Long neck. Long, sloping shoulder. Well-muscled, medium-length back. Long, muscular croup. Strong, well-made legs with large joints. Hard hooves.

Characteristics:
Known for its athletic ability, both under saddle and in harness.

What can I use it for?
Driving, dressage, jumping, competition and pleasure riding.

How tall is it?
16.1 to 17.2 hands

Where does it come from?
Germany, Europe

Temperament:
Quiet and even-tempered. Very trainable. Bold and willing.

Knabstrup

Lusitanos

Missouri Fox Trotters

Kiger Mustangs

Andalusians

Arabians

Wild Mustangs

Morgans

Rocky Mountain Horses

Thoroughbreds

Friesians

Lippizaners

Paso Finos

American Quarter Horses

Peruvian Paso Horses

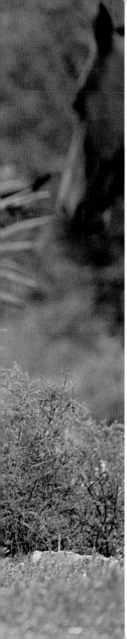

Boer Horses

Hanoverians

Tennessee Walking Horses

Andalusian

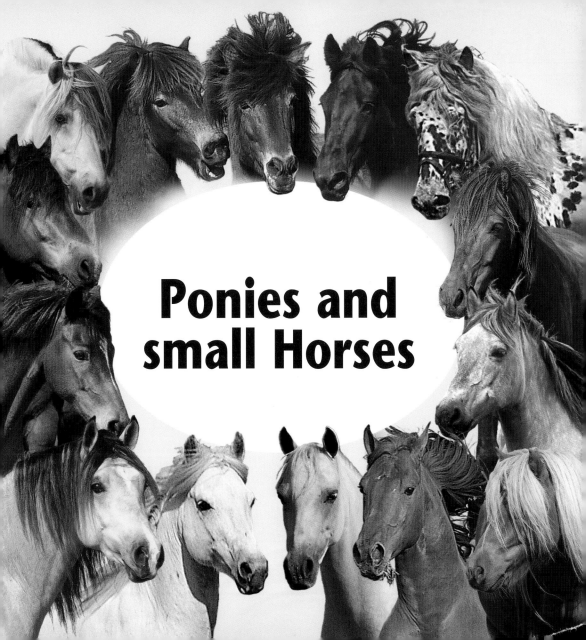

Ponies and small Horses

Altai

Background:
The harsh climate of the Altai Mountains influenced this breed which originated in Siberia many centuries ago. Named after the mountainous region, the Altai were used by tribesmen and nomads who relied on the horses to travel over extremely rugged terrain. Through the centuries, the Altai developed strong hearts and lungs and hard hooves, as they had to negotiate steep, rocky trails and dangerous river crossings. When the hardy Altai is crossed with larger breeds, the result is often a good performance horse.

Conformation:
Average-size, sometimes coarse head. Thick neck. Long, slightly dipped back. Well-muscled body. Short, strong legs. Very hard, tough hooves.

Characteristics:
Very sure-footed and sound. Can be solid colored chestnut, bay or black, or may be gray or spotted similar to Appaloosa coloring.

What can I use it for?
Riding, packing.

How tall is it?
14 to 14.3 hands

Where does it come from?
Siberia, Asia

Temperament:
Quiet and dependable.

American Shetland Pony

Background:

The Shetland Islands of Britain are the original home of the American Shetland Pony. Shetlands were first imported to the United States in the 1800s and a registry was established in 1888. Unlike the shorter, stouter British Shetland, the American Shetland is much more refined and elegant. This refinement is due to cross-breeding with Hackney Ponies, Arabians and Thoroughbreds. The American Shetland is very popular as a driving pony and also as a performance pony for children.

Conformation:

Attractive refined head with straight profile. Compact, smoothly-muscled body with good depth of girth. Slender, yet strong legs.

Characteristics:

Known for its elegance and high-stepping action.

What can I use it for?

Driving and halter classes. As a child's mount in English and Western disciplines.

How tall is it?

Up to 11.2 hands

Where does it come from?

United States, North America

Temperament:

Gentle, yet spirited and energetic.

American Miniature

Background:
Contrary to what some might think, the Miniature Horse is not a pony, but a scaled-down version of a regular-sized horse. Miniature horses first appeared in Europe in the 1600s where they were bred as pets for royal families. Some of the tiny horses were also used to work in the coal mines. Lady Estella Hope and her sisters continued breeding some of the original English bloodlines into the mid-1900s. Many of the smaller Miniature Horses in the United States today trace back to this Hope line. Found in at least 30 different countries around the world, Miniature Horses are popular as pets and for showing.

Conformation:
Petite, but harmonious and proportionate. Expressive head. Compact body. Short, strong legs.

Characteristics:
Agile and alert. Good family pet.

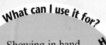

What can I use it for?
Showing in hand and driving, family pet.

How tall is it?
34 inches and under.

Where does it come from?
England, Europe

Temperament:
Friendly, gentle and affectionate.

Ariegeois

Background:
Also known as the "Chevel de Merens" or Merens Pony, the Ariegeois is a French pony which originated in the Pyrenees Mountains. This ancient breed's name hails from the Ariege River of that region. Roman horses, Percheron, Breton and Arabian bloodlines all contributed to the pony's heritage. The Ariegeois was first used as a pack pony and serves as a reliable work animal on mountain farms. Bearing a close resemblance to the Fell Pony, it also makes a stylish riding and harness pony. They are very easy keepers and don't require a lot of food and maintenance, and do well in cold weather.

Conformation:
Appealing, expressive head with wide-set eyes. Upright neck and shoulder. Flat withers. Long back. Short, sturdy legs with short cannon bones. May have slight feathering on heel area. Hard, sound hooves.

Characteristics:
Typically all black without white markings. Mane and tail are coarse and thick.

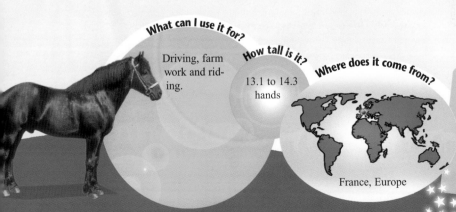

What can I use it for?
Driving, farm work and riding.

How tall is it?
13.1 to 14.3 hands

Where does it come from?
France, Europe

Temperament:
Spunky, but sensible. Willing worker.

Asturcon

Background:

Northern Spain is the birthplace of this rare, small breed of horse, also known as the Asturcon. They may have developed from crossing the Garrano Pony of northern Portugal and Spain with the Sorraia of Iberia. The ancient Celtic Pony might also have played a part in the breed's development. Asturcons were mentioned as early as 23 AD and became popular as ladies' mounts. They have a natural ambling gait that makes them comfortable to ride. Instead of trotting, the Asturcon alternately moves both legs on one side, as the pacer does.

Conformation:

Small, but rather heavy head with straight profile and small ears. Long, thin neck. Well-sloping shoulder. Moderately high withers with straight back. Sloping croup. Low-set tail. Very strong hooves.

Characteristics:

Ambling gait instead of a trot.

What can I use it for?

Riding and packing.

How tall is it?

11.2 to 12.2 hands

Where does it come from?

Spain, Europe

Temperament:

Calm and easy-going.

Australian Pony

Background:

Horses of English Thoroughbred and Spanish bloodlines first arrived by ship in Australia in 1788. Later, ponies from Timor and various Indonesian islands were imported, including the popular Sandalwood Pony. During the early 1800s, Arabians and a variety of European pony breeds were introduced, including the Exmoor, Shetland, New Forest, Highland, Connemara, Hackney and Welsh Mountain. All of these, but particularly the Welsh Mountain and the Arabian, contributed to the development of the Australian Pony, a popular show and riding pony.

Conformation:

Attractive head with large eyes and tapered muzzle. Good, sloping shoulder. Strong back. Powerful hindquarters. Strong, graceful legs with good bone. Tough, hard hooves.

Characteristics:

Very smooth, long stride for a pony.

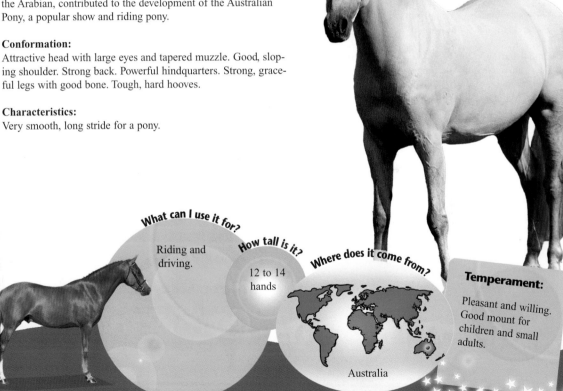

What can I use it for?
Riding and driving.

How tall is it?
12 to 14 hands

Where does it come from?
Australia

Temperament:
Pleasant and willing. Good mount for children and small adults.

139

Bardigiano Pony

Background:

Many horse lovers have never heard of this ancient Italian breed of mountain pony, as it is not commonly known outside its native country. Most likely descended from old Celtic Pony bloodlines, the Bardigiano Pony bears some resemblance to the rare Asturian and also the Exmoor Pony. Its mountain breeding makes the Bardigiano well-suited to working at high altitudes and in rugged terrain. They make ideal pack ponies and are also good for light draft work.

Conformation:

Short, attractive head with pony characteristics. Strongly-built, compact body. Deep girth. Short, upright shoulders. Well-muscled hindquarters. Short, strong legs. Tough hooves.

Characteristics:

Thick mane and tail. Very hardy and sure-footed.

What can I use it for?

Packing and light draft work.

How tall is it?

Up to 13 hands

Where does it come from?

Italy, Europe

Temperament:

Docile and easy-going.

140

Batak Pony

Background:
Native to the Indonesian island of Sumatra, the Batak Pony has some obvious Arabian characteristics. Sometimes referred to as the "Deli Pony," the Batak has been bred on the island for several centuries since the arrival of Dutch colonists. It is commonly used for crossbreeding to improve the quality of other pony breeds. The people of Sumatra often race their ponies, which are widely used for working and riding.

Conformation:
Delicate head. Slender and light-boned body. Straight back. Slim, but strong legs.

Characteristics:
Comes in wide variety of colors. Fine-haired mane and tail. Easy keeper.

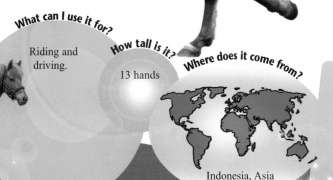

What can I use it for?

Riding and driving.

How tall is it?

13 hands

Where does it come from?

Indonesia, Asia

Temperament:

Gentle, but spirited.

Camargue Horse

Background:
Native to the flat salt marshes of southern France, the Camargue Horse is known for its hardiness. Often called the "horse of the sea," this ancient breed is believed to have descended from prehistoric horses that lived in the area. Born dark as foals, the horses eventually turn white. The Camargue is very agile and has long been used by the French ranch hands, or "guardians," to work the country's black fighting bulls. Some Camargue Horses still roam wild in France's salt water marshes where summers are scorchingly hot and winter months bring fierce, icy winds.

Conformation:
Plain, often heavy head with straight or slightly convex profile. Short, thick neck. Wide chest. Upright shoulders. Deep girth, strong short back. Powerful hindquarters and low-set tail. Short, sturdy, well-formed legs. Very tough hooves that are rarely shod.

Characteristics:
Sure-footed and hardy. Rough, short trot, but has a long, high-stepping walk. Easy keeper. Always gray in color.

What can I use it for?
Working cattle, trail and pleasure riding.

How tall is it?
13 to 14.2 hands

Where does it come from?
France, Europe

Temperament:
Courageous and even-tempered. Calm and easy-going attitude. Good family horse.

Caspian Pony

Background:

Although the Caspian Pony was rediscovered by the American traveler Louise L. Firouz on a trip to Iran in 1965, the breed is clearly an ancient one. In fact, the Caspian Pony, also referred to as the Caspian Horse, is said to be the oldest breed that still exists today, aside from the Asian Wild Horse. It is believed that the Arabian actually came into existence after the Caspian, and art from 500 B.C. shows small chariot horses that closely resemble the Caspian Pony. Although called a "pony" because of its size, the Caspian looks and moves more like a horse. They are known for their speed, natural jumping talent and ability to carry heavy loads. Only about 500 Caspians are thought to exist today.

Conformation:

Quality head with broad forehead and small, pointed ears. Long, arched neck. Good, sloping shoulder. Short back. Strong hindquarters. Slim, long legs with strong, dense cannon bones. Good hooves with plenty of heel.

Characteristics:

Known for its speed and graceful action. Often looks like a miniature Arabian.

What can I use it for?
Riding and driving.

How tall is it?
10 to 12 hands

Where does it come from?
Iran, Asia

Temperament:
Spirited, but docile. Affectionate and curious. Good children's pony.

Cayuse Indian Pony

Background:

Speed and endurance are prominent traits of this rugged breed, developed by the Cayuse Indian tribe of the American Northwest. Historians believe the breed's ancestors were French-Norman horses, including Percherons, which were imported to Canada in the 1600s. Traders brought these sturdy horses into American territories and bartered with Indians who then crossed them with horses of Spanish-Barb bloodlines originally brought to the Americas by Spanish explorers. By the 1800s, the Cayuse Indian Pony was recognized as a breed and respected for its stamina and hardiness.

Conformation:

Attractive head with straight profile. Wiry, well-muscled, stocky body. High withers. Fairly short back. Strong legs with unusually long cannon bones. Tough hooves.

Characteristics:

Easy keeper. Very sound and versatile. Often roan, pinto or Appaloosa-type coloring.

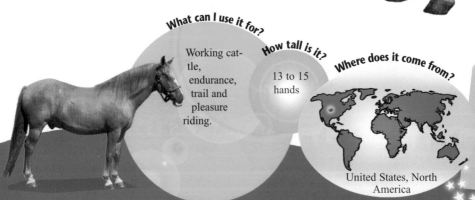

What can I use it for?
Working cattle, endurance, trail and pleasure riding.

How tall is it?
13 to 15 hands

Where does it come from?
United States, North America

Temperament:
Sensible and intelligent. Easy to work with.

Chincoteague Pony

Background:
In the 1600s, a Spanish ship sank off the coast of what would later become Virginia and Maryland in the United States. Seventeen horses of Arabian breeding escaped the sinking ship and swam ashore on the islands of Chincoteague and Assateague. Eating briar stems, seaweed and beach grass, the horses managed to survive, but became stunted in the harsh environment. Their descendants became the breed known today as the Chincoteague Pony. There are two groups of these unique ponies: the "Maryland Herd," owned by the Maryland Park Service, and the "Virginia Herd," owned by the Chincoteague Volunteer Fire Department. Each July, the Chincoteague Volunteer Fire Department rounds up their ponies and at low tide swims them across the channel to Virginia where the foals are sold at public auction.

Conformation:
Attractive head. Short to medium-length neck. Strong, compact and well-proportioned body. Strong, short legs. Tough hooves. Low-set tail. Thick mane and tail.

Characteristics:
Mostly pinto colored, with white combined with a solid color, such as black, bay, sorrel, palomino, or strawberry roan. Solid-colored black, sorrel and chestnut Chincoteague Ponies are also found. Easy keepers.

What can I use it for?
English and Western disciplines, trail riding and driving.

How tall is it?
Up to 14.2 hands

Where does it come from?
United States, North America

Temperament:
Intelligent, kind and pleasant-natured. Gentle, playful and people-oriented. Good child's mount.

Connemara

Background:

This popular, hardy pony takes its name from the rugged Western portion of its native Ireland known as Connemara. The breed's origins trace back at least 2,500 years when Celtic warriors brought ponies onto the island. Legend has it that Spanish ships sank off the coast in the 16th century, and the surviving Spanish Barb horses swam ashore and later bred with the wild native ponies. Crosses with Thoroughbreds, Arabians, Hackneys and Welsh Mountain Ponies contributed to the Connemara's fine reputation as a top quality performance pony with an ideal disposition and natural jumping ability.

Conformation:

Attractive head with well-defined jaw, wide forehead, and kind eyes. Long, graceful neck. Good sloping shoulder. Compact and sturdy body. Strong hindquarters and loins. High-set tail. Strong. sloping shoulder. Strong, well-made legs with dense bone. Good hooves.

Characteristics:

Sure-footed and agile, with excellent stamina. Easy keeper. Very versatile and known for its jumping ability. Can often outjump and outperform much larger horses.

What can I use it for?

Showing, hunter/jumper, endurance, dressage, eventing and driving. Also Western disciplines.

How tall is it?

13 to 15 hands

Where does it come from?

Ireland, Europe

Temperament:

Gentle and sensible. Willing and intelligent.

Dales Pony

Background:
Named after the upper dales of the slopes in northern England, the Dales Pony has the tough Scottish Galloway pony in its ancestry. Hardy and stout, the Dales Pony is known for its remarkable strength, even though it stands no more than 14.2 hands. Originally, the ponies were used as pack animals in lead and coal mines, as well as for farm work.
It was not unusual for them to cover 200 miles a week, all the while carrying a heavy load. Once popular in trotting races, the Dales Pony is a stylish trotter, both under saddle and in harness. A good mover with high action, the Dales is an excellent driving pony.

Conformation:
Straight profile with broad forehead and long forelock. Muscular neck. Short-coupled body with powerful, lengthy hindquarters. Sturdy legs with dense bone. Hard hooves with good shape. Silky feather on lower legs.

Characteristics:
Very sure-footed with tremendous stamina and agility. Easy keeper. Very hardy.
Black is the predominant color.

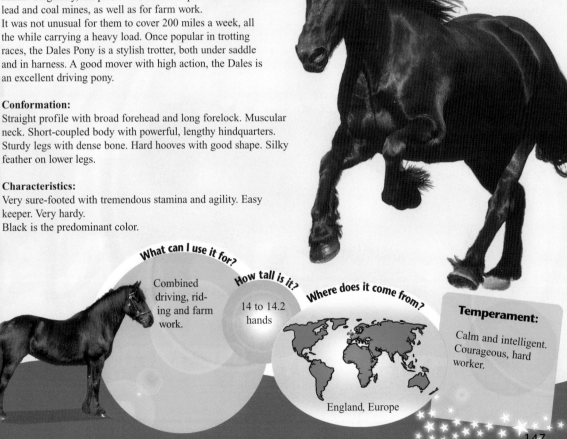

What can I use it for?
Combined driving, riding and farm work.

How tall is it?
14 to 14.2 hands

Where does it come from?
England, Europe

Temperament:
Calm and intelligent. Courageous, hard worker.

Dartmoor Pony

Background:
As early as 1012, there was reference to a Dartmoor Pony in the will of a Saxon Bishop. Much later, the ponies were routinely used as pack animals in England's tin mines. For centuries, a variety of other breeds were crossed with the Dartmoor. Arabian and Welsh Mountain Pony bloodlines have contributed to the Dartmoor's stylish appearance. Some of today's most influential bloodlines are the result of breeding by Miss Calmady-Hamlyn, Honorary Secretary of the Dartmoor Pony Society for over 30 years. A fine riding mount and good jumper, the Dartmoor has the sturdiness of a pony, but with quality and elegance.

Conformation:
Refined pony head with fine jaw, large nostrils and small, alert ears. Medium length neck. Well laid back, sloping shoulder. Deep girth. Well-muscled hindquarters. Short, strong cannon bones. Tough, sound hooves.

Characteristics:
Common colors are bay, brown, chestnut and roan. No pinto markings allowed. Full manes and tails. Free flowing movement without high-stepping action.

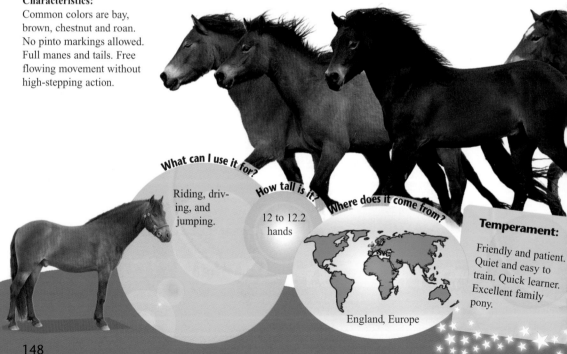

What can I use it for?
Riding, driving, and jumping.

How tall is it?
12 to 12.2 hands

Where does it come from?
England, Europe

Temperament:
Friendly and patient. Quiet and easy to train. Quick learner. Excellent family pony.

148

Eriskay Pony

Background:

Hailing from ancient Celtic and Norse bloodlines, the Eriskay Pony was named for the island of Eriskay, and is among the last surviving native ponies of the Western Isles of Scotland. They have a unique, dense coat that enables them to withstand the harshest of climates. Centuries ago, the Eriskay Pony was used to carry peat and seaweed, pull carts and do light farm work. Breed numbers declined greatly in the mid-1900s, but had increased somewhat by the end of the 1990s, although the Eriskay Pony is still considered rare. The Eriskay's ideal temperament makes it a fine family pony and it is useful for both driving and riding.

Conformation:

Large pony head. Thick neck. Compact, muscular overall build. Rounded hindquarters. Low-set tail. Short, sturdy legs. Light feathering on lower legs. Strong hooves.

Characteristics:

Very strong for their size. Foals are born dark and turn gray as they mature.

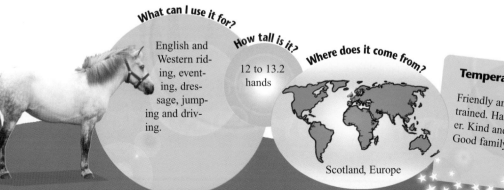

What can I use it for?

English and Western riding, eventing, dressage, jumping and driving.

How tall is it?

12 to 13.2 hands

Where does it come from?

Scotland, Europe

Temperament:

Friendly and easily trained. Hard worker. Kind and quiet. Good family pony.

149

Exmoor Pony

Background:

Considered the oldest of the British mountain ponies, the Exmoor's appearance has remained remarkably unchanged through centuries. A perfect example of "survival of the fittest," the Exmoor Pony is well suited to its native environment of the moorlands. Many of the breed's characteristics are the results of adapting to unforgiving weather and terrain. Their unique coloring with oatmeal shading has primitive origins and may have served as camouflage from predators, as it helps them blend into the moorlands. The Exmoor grows an unusual two-layer coat in the winter for protection from the cold, rain, snow and wind. Exceptionally strong for their small size, Exmoors make excellent harness ponies and mounts for children and small adults.

Conformation:

Definite pony head with broad forehead, small ears, large eyes and large lower jaw. Stocky, strong, compact body. Deep chest. Deep girth. Level back. Short legs. Extremely hard, tough hooves.

Characteristics:

Raised, fleshy rim above and below the eyes to divert rain water. Fan-like, thick, short hair at top of tail. Shades of brown with darker legs and oatmeal coloring around the muzzle, eyes, and sometimes under the body. Easy keeper. Hardy and agile. Great stamina and jumping ability.

What can I use it for?
Riding and driving.

How tall is it?
11.2 to 13.1 hands

Where does it come from?
England, Europe

Temperament:
Calm and easy-going. Independent attitude. Quick to learn. Willing worker.

Falabella

Background:
This well-known breed of miniature horse is named after the Falabella family of Buenos Aires, Argentina. The early ancestors were likely Andalusians that were brought to Latin America by Spanish explorers. The Falabella family developed the breed by crossing Shetland ponies with a tiny Thoroughbred stallion. They then took the smallest resulting horses and continued to selectively inbreed them to create a breed of miniature, or dwarf horses. The Falabella may be smaller than a pony, but it has the features of a horse. A registry was established in 1940, and the breed has since gained popularity as a pet around the world.

Conformation:
Petite, but harmonious, proportions. Fine, silky hair. Narrow, oval-shaped hooves.

Characteristics:
Known for longevity and may live into their 40s.

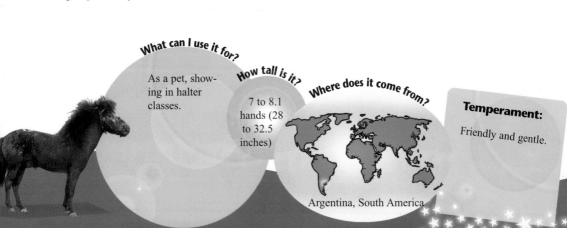

What can I use it for?
As a pet, showing in halter classes.

How tall is it?
7 to 8.1 hands (28 to 32.5 inches)

Where does it come from?
Argentina, South America

Temperament:
Friendly and gentle.

151

Fell Pony

Background:

Descended from a type of ancient Forest Pony, the Fell Pony originated in the harsh land of England's northern counties. The name comes from the "fells," or hills, of its native Britain, where some herds of wild ponies can still be found. The breed was strongly influenced by the Scottish Galloway. Originally, the Fell was used as a pack pony, but its excellent trot made it popular as a harness and riding pony. Fell Ponies are reliable work animals and well-suited to working in the rugged hill country. Fell bloodlines contributed to the creation of the modern Hackney Pony.

Conformation:

Attractive head with broad forehead, large eyes and short, alert ears. Fairly long neck. Sloping shoulder. Powerful, rounded hindquarters. Sturdy legs with heavy bone. Hard, strong hooves. Silky feather on lower leg.

Characteristics:

Black is the most common color, but bay, brown and gray are also found. Very long, thick manes and tails. Known for their hardiness and longevity

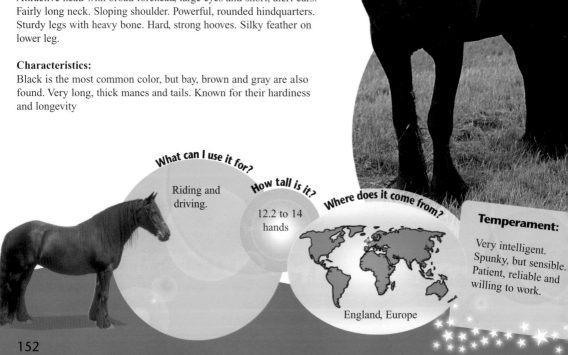

What can I use it for?
Riding and driving.

How tall is it?
12.2 to 14 hands

Where does it come from?
England, Europe

Temperament:
Very intelligent. Spunky, but sensible. Patient, reliable and willing to work.

Galiceno

Background:

Originally descended from the Sorraia and Garrano of the Iberian peninsula, the Galiceno takes its name from Spain's northwestern province of Galicia. When Spanish conqistadors invaded Mexico in the early 1500s, they brought these horses to North America. Small, but sturdy, the Galiceno became a popular breed in Mexico, used routinely for riding, ranch work and competition. The versatile Galiceno is known for its comfortable gaits and distinctive, ground-covering running walk, and has been a recognized breed since the 1950s.

Conformation:

Refined head with narrow, pointed ears, large eyes and small muzzle. Slender, slightly arched neck. Sloping shoulder. Short back with low-set tail. Compactly-built body. Slim, yet strong legs. Well-shaped, hard hooves.

Characteristics:

Known for its comfortable gaits and smooth running walk.

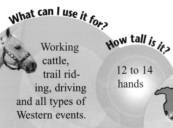

What can I use it for?
Working cattle, trail riding, driving and all types of Western events.

How tall is it?
12 to 14 hands

Where does it come from?
Mexico, North America

Temperament:

Intelligent and social. Gentle and easy to work with. Bonds well with people.

German Riding Pony

Background:

Not every rider looking to compete in equestrian sports wants a big warmblood. For that very reason, European breeders have created "sport ponies," which are athletic and more "horse-like" than many pony breeds. The Germany Riding Pony fits this description perfectly and riders love the breed for its heart and competitive spirit. Physically, the breed often resembles a small warmblood, and it has the same generous character and willingness. Germany Riding Ponies excel at dressage, jumping and cross-country.

Conformation:

Attractive, alert head that is more "horse-like" than "pony-like." Medium to long neck. Nice sloping shoulder. Good depth of girth. Strong, muscular back. Rounded, powerful hindquarters. Strong, well-made legs with good joints. Good hooves.

Characteristics:

Very athletic and known for its good gaits.

© Marielle Andersson Gueye

What can I use it for?

Dressage, jumping and most English riding disciplines.

How tall is it?

Up to 14.2 hands

Where does it come from?

Germany, Europe

Temperament:

Bold and kind. Eager to please.

Gotland Pony

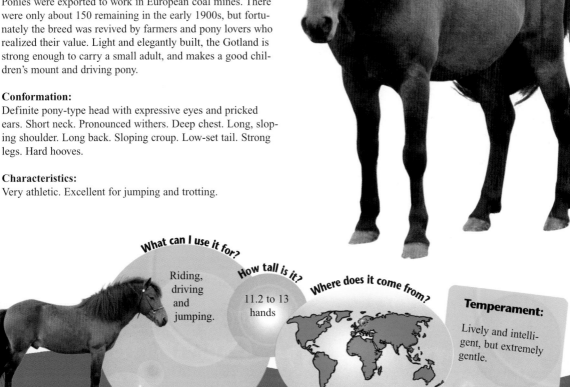

Background:

In its native Sweden, the Gotland Pony is also known as the Russ, and is thought to have descended from the ancient Tarpan horse. Free-roaming ponies lived for thousands of years in forested areas on the island of Gotland in the Baltic Sea, hence their name. During the 19th century, Gotland Ponies were exported to work in European coal mines. There were only about 150 remaining in the early 1900s, but fortunately the breed was revived by farmers and pony lovers who realized their value. Light and elegantly built, the Gotland is strong enough to carry a small adult, and makes a good children's mount and driving pony.

Conformation:

Definite pony-type head with expressive eyes and pricked ears. Short neck. Pronounced withers. Deep chest. Long, sloping shoulder. Long back. Sloping croup. Low-set tail. Strong legs. Hard hooves.

Characteristics:

Very athletic. Excellent for jumping and trotting.

What can I use it for?

Riding, driving and jumping.

How tall is it?

11.2 to 13 hands

Where does it come from?

Sweden, Europe

Temperament:

Lively and intelligent, but extremely gentle.

Haflinger

Background:

Named after the Tyrolean mountain village of Hafling, this breed was first documented in the 1870s, although regional artwork recorded the presence of these distinctive chestnut horses in the early 1800s. Originally part of Austria, the village of Hafling was turned over to Italy at the close of World War I. The breed was created by crossing a part-Arabian stallion with Austrian mountain mares. Haflingers were once used primarily for packing in mountainous areas, but are now popular for both riding and driving. They are easy keepers and it is common for them to live into their late 30s.

Conformation:

Refined, expressive head with large eyes. Medium length neck. Sloping shoulder. Muscular body with plenty of bone. Deep girth. Rounded croup. Strong, well-made legs with broad knees and powerful hocks. Hard, tough hooves.

Characteristics:

Always chestnut in color, ranging from golden to chocolate, with a flaxen or white mane and tail.

What can I use it for?

Driving, farm work, packing, trail riding, therapeutic riding and showing in numerous disciplines.

How tall is it?

12.2 to 14.3 hands

Where does it come from?

Austria, Europe

Temperament:

Laid back, friendly and willing.

Highland Pony

Background:
A native of Scotland, the Highland Pony has a long history.
Bloodlines that contributed to the Highland include the
Arabian, Spanish and French breeds, as well as other breeds
of British ponies. The sure-footed Highland Pony was a
popular work animal in Scotland's mountainous areas.
Steady and reliable, they are also used for packing game
out of the hills and for pony trekking. Their sturdy build
is often more like that of a horse with short legs, than a
pony

Conformation:
Attractive head with broad forehead. Well-muscled neck. Heavy
build with plenty of bone and substance. Powerful hindquarters.
High-set tail. Stout legs. Good hooves.

Characteristics:
Very sure-footed and able to carry heavy weight. Wide range of colors. White markings are uncommon. Ponies with dun coloring often
have primitive markings such as dorsal back stripe and zebra bars on the
legs.

What can I use it for?
Riding and driving, trekking and pack-ing.

How tall is it?
13 to 14.2 hands

Where does it come from?
Scotland, Europe

Temperament:
Steady, quiet and agreeable. Good all-around family pony.

Hokkaido

Background:
Domestic horses were found in Japan as early as the 6th century or before. Once used in warfare, they were later employed as pack animals, and ridden by upper class families. Named after the island of Hokkaido, this breed's ancestors may have come from China originally.

Considered a rare breed, the Hokkaido is also known as the Dosanko, which is a term of endearment in Japan. They are thought to have developed from several local breeds imported to Japan in the 15th century. Many are allowed to run loose on the grazing areas and are rounded up annually. Strong for its small size, the Hokkaido is useful in mountainous areas where vehicles cannot travel.

Conformation:
Fairly large head for body size. Short neck tends to be carried horizontally. Upright shoulder. Flat withers. Wide croup. Light-boned legs. Good hooves.

Characteristics:
Thick mane. Found in most solid colors, often roan. White markings not common. Many are natural pacers. Extremely hardy and able to do well in harsh conditions.

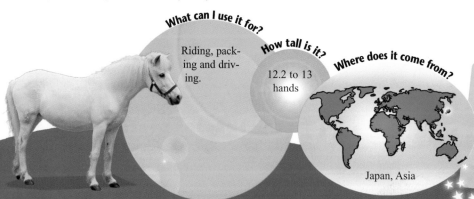

What can I use it for?
Riding, packing and driving.

How tall is it?
12.2 to 13 hands

Where does it come from?
Japan, Asia

Temperament:
Easy-going and willing.

158

Hucul

Background:

The Hucul dates back to the 13th century and many believe it descended from a cross of Mongolian horses and the ancient wild Tarpan. This tough pony breed is native to the Carpathian Mountains of Eastern Europe, and is sometimes referred to as the Carpathian Pony. Its mountain heritage and rugged environment created a hearty and durable animal, well-suited for use as a sure-footed pack and riding pony. Breeders created different types of Hucul, from a light type used for packing and riding, to a heavier draft type pony. Due to border changes throughout history, both Poland and Romania lay claim to the Hucul's development.

Conformation:

Expressive head with large eyes and small, alert ears. Muscular neck. Low withers. Deep, broad chest. Short and compact build. Strong legs. Excellent, hard feet.

Characteristics:

Rectangular-shaped body is slightly longer than its height at the withers.
Hardy and resistant to disease. Very sure-footed in rough terrain.

What can I use it for?
Riding, driving and packing.

How tall is it?
12.3 to 13.2 hands

Where does it come from?
Poland/Romania, Europe

Temperament:
Willing and gentle.

Icelandic Horse

Background:

Although pony-sized, the Icelandic Horse is never referred to as a pony in its native island country of Iceland. The Vikings brought horses with them when they settled the "land of fire and ice" in the late 9th century. The versatile Icelandic Horse is a highly regarded and popular mount, thanks to its hardiness and unique gaits. In addition to the basic walk, trot and canter, the Icelandic is known for the tolt and the pace. The tolt is the breed's specialty and is an extremely smooth, four-beat gait in which the forelegs are lifted high and the hind legs come well under the body. It is similar to a running walk or rack. At the speedy two-beat pace, the horse moves both legs on each side forward and back together. Although slow to mature, the Icelandic is long lived and often ridden well into old age.

Conformation:

Large head. Short, strong neck. Upright shoulder. Compact body. Clean, short legs with short cannon bones. Powerful hocks. Good large hooves.

Characteristics:

Great strength and endurance. Despite its size, easily able to carry a full-grown man. Known for its smooth tolt and fast pacing gait.

What can I use it for?

Showing, driving, riding, dressage, jumping, eventing, trekking, and farm work.

How tall is it?

12 to 13.2 hands

Where does it come from?

Iceland, Europe

Temperament:

Self-assured and intelligent. Docile and enthusiastic. Willing worker.

Java Pony

Background:
Named after its native island of Java, this slightly-built pony is mainly used for pulling carts carrying either passengers or goods through city streets. Incredibly strong for its size, the Java Pony is said to have descended from the Mongolian wild horse, and has Arabian and Barb blood in its early history. Found in all colors, this hardy Indonesian pony has adapted well to the island's tropical heat. Java Ponies are typically light-boned, but willing and almost tireless workers.

Conformation:
Small head, slight build. Light-boned legs. Often cow-hocked.

Characteristics:
Great stamina. Able to pull heavy weights, despite their slight build.

What can I use it for?
Pulling two-wheeled carts, general all-around work. Can also be ridden.

How tall is it?
12.2 hands

Where does it come from?
Indonesia, Asia

Temperament:
Quiet and willing. Hard worker.

Kiso

Background:
Records show that this pony-sized horse was raised in the Kiso region of Japan's Nagano Prefecture as early as the 6th century. At one point, thousands of horses were supposedly raised there as cavalry mounts for warrior Kiso Yoshinaka's army. The Kiso may have descended from horses of Central Asia or Mongolia. Japanese horses have been used widely on farms and for transportation. Once used for agricultural purposes, today the Kiso is a rare breed that is used in Japanese festivals and for riding.

Conformation:
Rather large head. Flat withers. Upright shoulder. Short body with robust build. Low-set tail. Hard, well-shaped hooves.

Characteristics:
Some have a dorsal back stripe.

What can I use it for?
Riding.

How tall is it?
13 hands

Where does it come from?
Japan, Asia

Temperament:
Very calm, friendly and curious. Intelligent, independent and can be quite stubborn.

Konik

Background:
Popular throughout its native country of Poland, the Konik descended from the ancient Tarpan. As the breed developed, Arabian bloodlines were added to bring some refinement. The Konik has been bred in Poland for centuries where it is used by farmers as a working pony and also for riding. Robust and easy to work with, its name literally means "small horse" in Polish.

Conformation:
Large head. Short, strong neck. Upright shoulder. Low withers. Deep girth. Broad, well-proportioned body. Strong legs.

Characteristics:
Typically dun-colored with dorsal stripe down back. Known for its longevity.

What can I use it for?
Farm work and riding.

How tall is it?
12 to 13.1 hands

Where does it come from?
Poland, Europe

Temperament:
Self-reliant and quiet. Good-natured, willing worker.

163

Landais

Background:

Hailing from France, the Landais is one of three pony breeds native to that country, and is likely a descendent of the ancient Tarpan. Once semi-wild, the Landais has been crossbred through the centuries with Arabian, Anglo-Arab and Barb stallions. The breed came dangerously close to extinction after World War II, but breeders who fancied the Landais came to the rescue and crossed the remaining ponies with Welsh Section B stallions, and also with Arabians. Today's Landais is hardy but elegant, and well-suited as both a harness and riding pony for young riders.

Conformation:

Square, slender, attractive head with small, pointed ears. Thick neck. Prominent withers. Sloping shoulder. Short, straight back. High-set tail. Well-muscled legs.

Characteristics:

Appearance often resembles a miniature Arabian. Easy keeper.

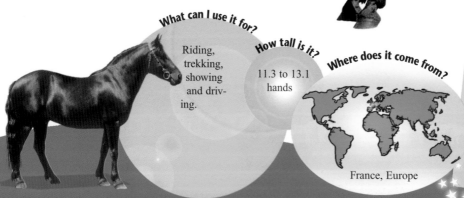

What can I use it for?

Riding, trekking, showing and driving.

How tall is it?

11.3 to 13.1 hands

Where does it come from?

France, Europe

Temperament:

Docile and intelligent. Good children's pony.

Misaki

Background:

A native Japanese breed, the Misaki Horse originated in the late 1600s in the Miyazaki Prefecture around Cape Toi. The word Misaki means "cape" and Cape Toi is now a popular tourist spot. Like other Japanese breeds, the Misaki Horse is relatively small, very hardy, and can live in harsh weather conditions. Although often referred to as a horse, the Misaki is actually pony-sized and runs wild in the Cape Toi area, where it is rounded up once a year to be vaccinated and checked for health concerns. The Misaki is considered a rare breed and has been designated a "National Natural Treasure" in Japan.

Conformation:

Fairly large head. Neck is typically carried horizontally. Thick mane. Short back. Croup is wide at top and narrows toward the legs. Slender legs. Extremely tough hooves.

Characteristics:

Usually black or bay. White markings are uncommon.

What can I use it for?
Riding and packing.

How tall is it?
12.2 to 13.2 hands

Where does it come from?
Japan, Asia

Temperament:
Generally easy-going and quiet.

165

New Forest Pony

Background:
Centuries ago, herds of wild ponies roamed across Britain, and in 1060, Canute's Forest Law makes mention of ponies living in the forests along the English coast. Welsh mares were later introduced in an attempt to upgrade the bloodlines, but perhaps the most notable influence came in the 1760s from the Thoroughbred stallion Marske, sire of the outstanding racehorse, Eclipse. Other British pony breeds contributed bloodlines to the New Forest Pony, including the Galloway, Dales, Fells, Dartmoor, Exmoor, and Welsh, as well as the Arabian. Today's New Forest Pony makes an agile and reliable riding pony for children and small adults.

Conformation:
Head may be either "horse-like" or "pony-like." Long, sloping shoulder. Deep body. Powerful, well-muscled hindquarters. Sturdy, straight legs. Tough, hard hooves.

Characteristics:
Long stride for a pony. Prominent colors are bay, brown and gray.

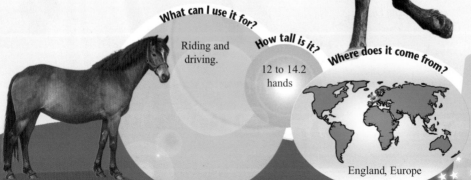

What can I use it for?
Riding and driving.

How tall is it?
12 to 14.2 hands

Where does it come from?
England, Europe

Temperament:
Intelligent. Agreeable, easy-going and willing to please. Good family pony.

166

Norwegian Fjord Horse

Background:
One of the oldest breeds in the world, the Norwegian Fjord Horse looks much like the horses found in cave drawings many thousands of years ago. It is likely related to the primitive Przewalski's Horse, also known as the Asian Wild Horse. Historians believe the Fjord was domesticated around 2,000 B.C. Used by the Vikings as a war horse, the Fjord was later used by Norwegian farmers as a general purpose work horse. Although often pony-sized, the Fjord is referred to as a horse. Most Fjord Horses are dun-colored, and usually have a dark dorsal stripe running from forelock to tail, in addition to zebra stripes on their legs.

Conformation:
Medium-sized head with flat, wide forehead. Profile may be straight or slightly dished. Well-muscled, thick, crested neck. Low withers. Compact body. Deep girth. Short to medium-length back. Broad, strong hindquarters. Muscular, rounded croup. Short, strong legs with substantial bone. Dense, hard, black hooves.

Characteristics:
Mane is cut short in a crescent shape so it stands erect, emphasizing the dark center hair.

What can I use it for?
Draft work, riding and driving, mountain trekking, riding schools and therapeutic riding groups.

How tall is it?
13.2 to 15 hands

Where does it come from?
Norway, Europe

Temperament:
Gentle, willing worker.

Northland Horse

Background:
This Norwegian pony breed is referred to as a horse in its native country. Its ancestors are northern pony types of Mongolian and Tarpan blood. The northern pony type also includes the Konik (a Polish pony) and the Celtic ponies Exmoor, Iceland and Shetland. The modern Northland Horse owes much to a selected stallion named Rimfakse. In the 1940s Rimfakse was judged to be a typical Northland and was used to improve existing stock.

Conformation:
A stocky pony with short body and a thick neck. It bears a strong resemblance to the Iceland Pony, but the head is smaller.

Characteristics:
Usually dark colored. The hooves are exceptionally hard.

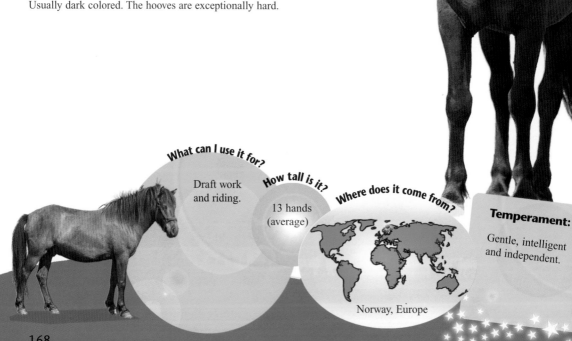

What can I use it for?
Draft work and riding.

How tall is it?
13 hands (average)

Where does it come from?
Norway, Europe

Temperament:
Gentle, intelligent and independent.

Padang Pony

Background:
The Indonesian island of Sumatra is home to this pony, which was bred by Dutch settlers. The Batak, another Indonesian pony, was crossed with Arabian bloodlines to create the Padang Pony. Despite its slight build, the Padang is very sturdy and hard-working for its size. It has been used to upgrade other Indonesian pony breeds, such as the Java.

Conformation:
Refined, smallish head. Slight overall build. Slim legs with long cannon bones. Tough hooves.

Characteristics:
Usually bay or brown.

What can I use it for?
Riding and harness work.

How tall is it?
12.2 to 14.2 hands

Where does it come from?
Indonesia, Asia

Temperament:
Spirited, but easy-going. Willing, tireless worker.

Pindos Pony

Background:
Also known as the Thessalonian, the Pindos Pony originated in the areas of Thessaly and Epirus in Greece. The pony descended from the old Thessalonian breed, as well as other strains that no longer exist. Although not beautiful, the Pindos Pony is known for its hardiness and endurance. They are used for light draft work on farms and as pack ponies in mountainous areas, as well as for riding and driving.

Conformation:
Long, sometimes coarse head. Narrow body. Long back. Typically poor hindquarters. High-set tail. Slender legs. Hard, narrow hooves.

Characteristics:
Easy keeper. Good stamina. Typically black, bay or brown.

What can I use it for?
Riding, driving and packing.

How tall is it?
12 to 13 hands

Where does it come from?
Greece, Europe

Temperament:
Good worker, but can be stubborn.

Pony of the Americas

Background:

A relatively new breed, the Pony of the Americas (POA) became recognized in the mid-1950s through the efforts of Les Broomhower of Iowa, who originally bred Shetland Ponies. The breed's foundation stallion, Black Hand, was the result of crossing a Shetland stallion with an Arabian/Appaloosa mare. Over time, the Shetland cross lost popularity and the bloodlines of larger ponies, such as Welsh and Indian ponies, as well as Arabs, Quarter Horses, and Appaloosas were used. As a result, the POA has the size of a pony, but the refined and stylish look of a small horse. The ideal POA resembles a miniature Arabian/Quarter Horse cross with Appaloosa coloring and characteristics.

Conformation:

Small, attractive, expressive head which may be somewhat dished, thanks to Arabian bloodlines. Well-muscled body similar to Quarter Horse in appearance. Strong legs. Hard, sound hooves.

Characteristics:

Same coat patterns as the Appaloosa breed with the blanket pattern one of the most common. Skin is mottled or parti-colored, like the Appaloosa. White sclera encircling one or both eyes. Light and dark vertically striped hooves found in many POAs.

What can I use it for?

Trail and endurance riding, ranch work, English and Western showing.

How tall is it?

11.2 to 13.2 hands

Where does it come from?

United States, North America

Temperament:

Gentle, intelligent and easy to train. Excellent mount for children and small adults.

Pottock Pony

Background:

Descended from the ancient Tarpan, the Pottock Pony is native to France's mountainous Basque region, along the border of Spain. Crossing breeding with Welsh Section B and Arabian stallions helped improve this wild breed. Still considered semi-wild in some areas, Pottock Ponies are rounded up each winter and either sold or returned to the mountains as breeding stock. They have been used for many years as pack animals along mountain trails. Before World War II, they were popular with smugglers who used Pottock Ponies to pack their contraband goods. Today, the Pottock is used both for driving and riding.

Conformation:

Small head with straight profile, but may have small concave area between eyes. Short neck. Straight shoulder. Long, straight back. Short hindquarters. Sloping croup. Fairly high-set tail. Fine, slender legs. Small, hard hooves.

Characteristics:

Very sure-footed and known for its endurance.

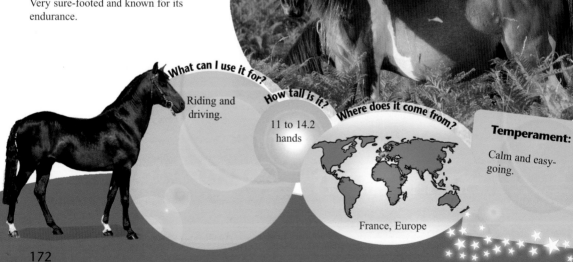

What can I use it for?
Riding and driving.

How tall is it?
11 to 14.2 hands

Where does it come from?
France, Europe

Temperament:
Calm and easy-going.

Przewalski's Horse

Background:

Also known as the Asian Wild Horse, this sturdy, pony-like horse was named after the Russian colonel who discovered it in 1879. Although Przewalski was given credit for discovering the Asian Wild Horse, herds had been reported decades earlier. At the time of their discovery, they were found in the Gobi Desert region of Mongolia, but once roamed far and wide across the grasslands of central Asia. Today, captive Przewalski's Horses are bred in various zoos with the hopes of some day re-establishing the species in the wild.

Conformation:

Large heavy head with convex profile. Coarse upright mane with little or no forelock. Straight back. Hindquarters similar to mule or donkey. Dorsal stripe down back. Black lower legs that may have zebra striping. Dark, plumed coarse tail.

Characteristics:

Dun-colored with black legs.

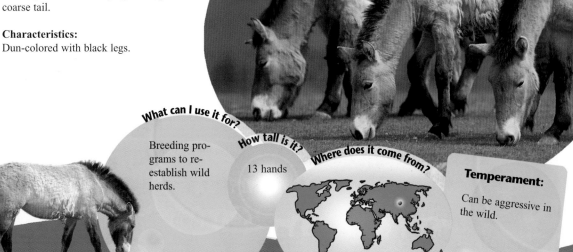

What can I use it for?

Breeding programs to re-establish wild herds.

How tall is it?

13 hands

Where does it come from?

Mongolia, Asia

Temperament:

Can be aggressive in the wild.

Sable Island Pony

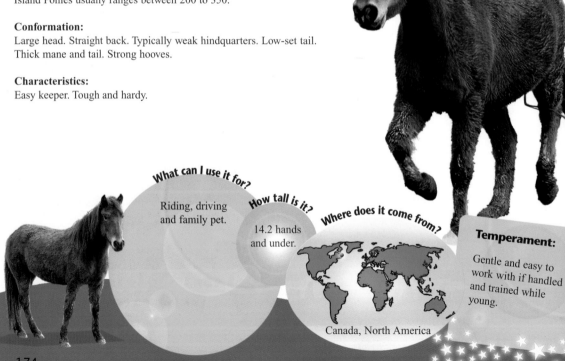

Background:
A barren, sandy island off the coast of Nova Scotia, Canada, is home to the Sable Island Pony. Horses of French stock first came to Nova Scotia in the early 1600s, and were a mixture of several breeds. They were later crossed with stallions from the American colonies. Legend has it that some of these horses were turned loose on Sable Island. Another popular tale is that horses survived a shipwreck and swam ashore on the island. Whatever their background, the Sable Island Pony has roamed there for some 400 years and has been the topic of numerous books, articles and documentaries. Among the few wild horse populations that are entirely unmanaged, the number of Sable Island Ponies usually ranges between 200 to 350.

Conformation:
Large head. Straight back. Typically weak hindquarters. Low-set tail. Thick mane and tail. Strong hooves.

Characteristics:
Easy keeper. Tough and hardy.

What can I use it for?
Riding, driving and family pet.

How tall is it?
14.2 hands and under.

Where does it come from?
Canada, North America

Temperament:
Gentle and easy to work with if handled and trained while young.

Sandalwood Pony

Background:
Originating on the Indonesian islands of Sumba and Sumbawa, the Sandalwood Pony takes its name from the aromatic wood that is a main export of these islands. Dutch colonists brought in Arabian stock hundreds of years ago, which was used to improve the Sandalwood. Speedy and agile, the Sandalwood Pony was used for racing in Thailand. They have been imported to Australia, where they became popular as children's mounts, and to Malaysia where they were often crossed with Thoroughbreds. The Sandalwood is considered the largest of the Indonesian pony breeds.

Conformation:
Refined, small head with large eyes and small, alert ears. Short neck. Long, narrow back. High-set tail. Slender legs. Very hard, durable hooves.

Characteristics:
Known for its speed and agility. Comes in all colors.

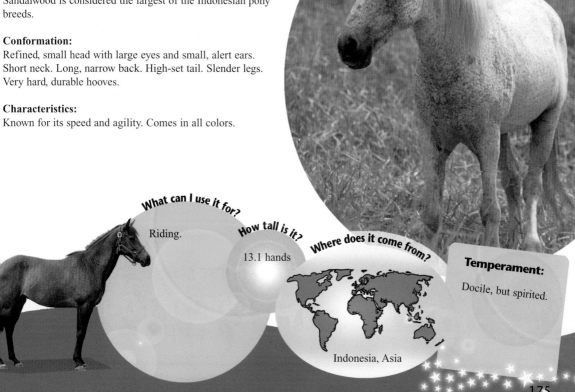

What can I use it for?
Riding.

How tall is it?
13.1 hands

Where does it come from?
Indonesia, Asia

Temperament:
Docile, but spirited.

Shetland Pony

Background:
The smallest of the British pony breeds, the popular Shetland Pony is named after the Shetland Islands off the northern coast of Scotland where it originated some 2,000 years ago. Although small in size, the Shetland Pony is very strong and hardy. They were used extensively as "pit ponies" to haul cars of coal in the coal mines during the 1800s and early 1900s. Shetlands were also used to haul peat and seaweed, which were used as fuel and fertilizer. Resilient and tough, they are known for their thick, shaggy winter coats. The Shetland remains a beloved children's mount and driving pony.

Conformation:
Medium-sized head with well-shaped muzzle and prominent jaw. Full-bodied with short legs. Sloping shoulder. Short, broad back. Well-made hindquarters.

Characteristics:
Substantial mane and tail. Very hardy. Common colors are black and dark brown.

What can I use it for?
Driving, riding, and showing in halter classes.

How tall is it?
9.3 to 10.2 hands

Where does it come from?
Scotland, Europe

Temperament:
Independent, sensible and docile.

Skyros Pony

Background:
The island of Skyros in the Aegean Sea is home to the Skyros Pony, also known as the Skyrian Horse or Skyrian Pony. These may well be the naturally diminutive mounts carved on the Parthenon frieze. The Skyros Pony has been used for agricultural purposes for centuries, although no one is quite sure how they first arrived on the island. Unfortunately, the law does not permit the ponies to leave the island, and at last count there were less than 150 in existence. If something is not done to save them, the rare Skyros Pony is likely to become extinct.

Conformation:
Small, fine head with wide forehead and wide-set, prominent eyes. Straight shoulder. Compact body. Poorly developed hindquarters. Tough, black hooves.

Characteristics:
Known for its stamina and ability to carry weight.

What can I use it for?
Riding and light farm work.

How tall is it?
11 to 12 hands

Where does it come from?
Greece, Europe

Temperament:
Good-natured.

Sorraia

Background:

An ancient breed, the Sorraia likely descended from the Tarpan and Asian Wild Horse, and still retains its primitive look. Indeed, prehistoric cave drawings of horses that closely resemble the Sorraia have been found. Native to the Iberian Peninsula, Sorraias were among the horses brought to the New World by Spanish explorers. Their bloodlines can be found in numerous North and South American breeds today, and DNA testing of some American mustangs shows they trace directly back to the Sorraia. The pony-sized Sorraia is probably an ancestor of the Andalusian, Lusitano and Barb. Today, there are not many of the hardy little Sorraias left.

Conformation:

Refined head with wide forehead and convex profile, sometimes called a "ram's" head. Strong neck. Prominent withers. Long shoulder. Deep, narrow chest. Straight back. Sloping croup. Short, slender legs with fairly long cannon bones and well-defined tendons. Tough hooves.

Characteristics:

May be gaited. Always dun or grulla with bi-colored mane and tail. May have dorsal stripe down back and zebra stripes on legs.

What can I use it for?

General riding and working cattle.

How tall is it?

13.3 to 14.3 hands

Where does it come from?

Iberian Peninsula, Europe

Temperament:

Easy-going with a strong sense of self-preservation.

Sumba Pony

Background:

This Indonesian pony is named after its native island of Sumba in the Flores Sea. First visited by Europeans in the 1520s, the island came under Dutch control in the mid-1860s. Agile and speedy, the Sumba Pony is primitive in appearance and resembles the Mongolian horse and the Tarpan. Sometimes referred to as the Sumbawa, the Sumba Pony is extremely hardy and tough, and can carry the weight of a large pack or a full-grown man, despite its small size. The finest Sumbas are chosen for ceremonial dances with bells attached to their legs. These ancient horse dancing traditions can also be found in parts of Central Asia and India.

Conformation:

Small head. Short neck. Small, lightly-built body. Strong back. Sturdy legs.

Characteristics:

Usually dun-colored with dorsal stripe. May have zebra stripes on legs.

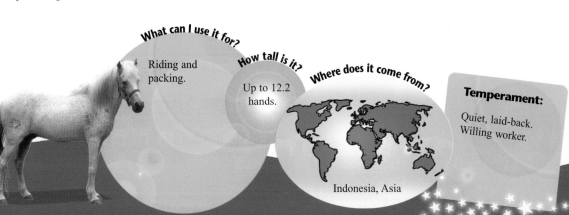

What can I use it for?
Riding and packing.

How tall is it?
Up to 12.2 hands.

Where does it come from?
Indonesia, Asia

Temperament:
Quiet, laid-back. Willing worker.

179

Tokara

Background:
A native Japanese breed, the small Tokara Horse was once found throughout the country's Kagoshima region. Bred on Tokara Island, numbers of the pony-sized Tokara decreased dramatically as a result of World War II. In 1950, a Dr. Shigeyuki Hayashida found a small herd of the horses still living on the Tokara Islands. They may have been brought to the islands in the late 1800s for use as farm and pack horses. The Tokara is considered a rare breed and today there are only about 100 to 120 remaining. They are found in several natural parks in the Kagoshima Prefecture, where they have been designated a Natural Treasure.

Conformation:
Large head with straight profile. Short, thick neck carried horizontally. Upright shoulder. Compact body. Short back. Sloping croup. Slender legs. Tough, hard hooves.

Characteristics:
Easy keeper.

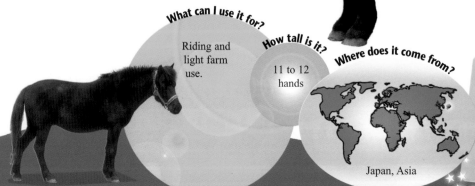

What can I use it for?
Riding and light farm use.

How tall is it?
11 to 12 hands

Where does it come from?
Japan, Asia

Temperament:
Calm and independent.

180

Welsh Mountain Pony - Section A

Background:

Hardy, enduring, and beloved by many, the Welsh Mountain Pony hails from the mountain country of Wales where it has lived for centuries. The Welsh Pony traces its heritage back to the days of the Romans and bears obvious signs of Arabian bloodlines. It is likely that some Thoroughbred and Hackney blood may also have been added. The Welsh Pony developed a distinct appearance and is known to pass on its best qualities when crossed with other breeds. The "Section A" is the smallest of the Welsh Ponies, and is a highly popular riding and driving pony.

Conformation:

Small, refined head with wide forehead, large eyes and neat, pointed ears. Profile may be slightly dished and muzzle is small. Good length of neck to proportions. Sloping shoulder. Well-defined withers. Deep girth. Muscular hindquarters. High-set tail. Elegant, well-made legs with strong, dense bone and good joints.

Characteristics:

Known for its great soundness, endurance and versatility.

What can I use it for?

Riding and driving, pleasure and trail riding.

How tall is it?

12 hands and under

Where does it come from?

Wales, Europe

Temperament:

Intelligent, kind and willing. Ideal child's pony.

Welsh Pony - Section B

Background:
Bred to perform, the Welsh Pony Section B is larger and longer striding than the smaller Section A. Most of the Welsh Mountain Pony's finest attributes, however, remain the same. The Section B was originally a cross between the Welsh Mountain Pony and the smaller Welsh Cob. Its natural jumping ability, soundness and superb disposition make the Welsh Pony a standout in the show ring and as a pleasure mount.

Conformation:
Small, refined head with wide forehead, large eyes and neat, pointed ears. Profile may be slightly dished and muzzle is small. Long, slightly arched neck. Sloping shoulder. Well-defined withers. Deep girth. Muscular hindquarters. High-set tail. Elegant, well-made legs with strong, dense bone and good joints.

Characteristics:
Known as a top class riding pony for both performance and pleasure.

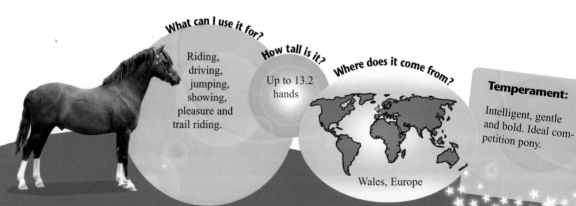

What can I use it for?
Riding, driving, jumping, showing, pleasure and trail riding.

How tall is it?
Up to 13.2 hands

Where does it come from?
Wales, Europe

Temperament:
Intelligent, gentle and bold. Ideal competition pony.

Welsh Cob - Section C

Background:
Centuries ago, the Welsh Pony of Cob Type was developed by crossing the Welsh Mountain Pony with horses of Spanish origin. Bloodlines of the Norfolk Trotter, Yorkshire Coach Horse and Hackney also contributed to the development of the Welsh Cob, and as a result of the Crusades, Arabian blood was also introduced. Although originally bred as a sure-footed work horse, the swift Welsh Cob was also known for its outstanding ability to trot long distances. Crossing the Welsh Cob with the Thoroughbred yields an ideal competition horse for both riding and driving. The Welsh Cob Section C is the smaller of the two Welsh Cob types.

Conformation:
Quality pony head with broad forehead, large eyes and neat, well-set ears. Slightly arched neck. Sloping shoulder. Deep girth. Compact, powerful body. Muscular hindquarters. Short, strong loins. Muscular, short legs with strong, dense bone and good joints.

Characteristics:
Known for its excellent action and soundness.

What can I use it for?
Riding and driving, jumping, hunting, showing, pleasure and trail riding.

How tall is it?
Up to 13.2 hands

Where does it come from?

Wales, Europe

Temperament:
Intelligent, kind and courageous. Fine pony for both adults and children.

Welsh Cob - Section D

Background:

Long ago in the 15th century, the hardy Welsh Cob was used by knights to lead their magnificent war horses. Though smaller than the mighty battle horses, they had to match the big horses' stride at the trot. Even today, the Welsh Cob is known for its grand trot. They were also used as military mounts, to pull heavy equipment, and as reliable riding horses for rural doctors. The Welsh Cob Section D is the larger of the two Welsh Cob types and has evolved into a popular competition horse, both under saddle and in harness.

Conformation:

Quality pony head with broad forehead, large eyes and neat, well-set ears. Slightly arched neck. Strong, laid-back shoulder. Deep girth. Compact, powerful body. Muscular hindquarters. Short, strong loins. Muscular, short legs with strong, dense bone and good joints. Powerful hocks. Some silky feathering on lower leg. Dense hooves.

Characteristics:

Strong and hardy. Great endurance.

What can I use it for?

Riding and driving, dressage, hunting, combined training, combined driving, jumping, showing, pleasure and trail riding.

How tall is it?

Over 13.2 hands – no upper height limit.

Where does it come from?

Wales, Europe

Temperament:

Intelligent, sensible and bold. Ideal driving or riding horse for adults and children.

Dartmoor Pony

Norwegian Fjord Horses

Chincoteague Ponies

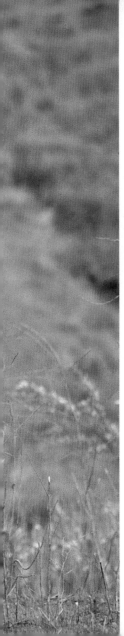

Icelandic Horses

Welsh Ponies

Camargue Horses

Dartmoor Ponies

New Forest Ponies

Sable Island Pony

Northland Horse

Shetland Ponies

Hucul

Heavy Horses

American Cream Draft

Background:
The only draft breed to originate in the United States, the American Cream Draft Horse became a recognized breed in 1950. Nearly all of today's Creams trace back to a cream-colored draft mare named "Old Granny," who was born between 1900 and 1905. Harry Lakin, a well-known breeder, purchased the mare at an auction in Iowa in 1911. She produced a number of cream-colored foals for him, and became the first registered American Cream. Considered a medium to heavy draft horse, the American Cream Draft Horse carries the bloodlines of several breeds, including Belgian, Shire, and Percheron.

Conformation:
Attractive head. Thick, muscular neck. Wide chest. Deep girth. Compact, well-muscled, powerful body. Strong, rounded hindquarters. Short, strong legs with broad joints.

Characteristics:
Rich cream-colored coat with white mane and tail, pink skin, and amber or clear red-brown eyes. Foals are born with nearly white eyes, which turn darker when they are yearlings. Breed is very uniform in body type.

What can I use it for?
Farm work, showing in harness, pleasure driving and carriage businesses.

How tall is it?
15.2 to 16.3 hands

Where does it come from?
United States, North America

Temperament:
Pleasant, friendly disposition. Willing worker.

Ardennais

Background:

Also known as the Ardennes, this ancient draft breed takes its name from the Ardennes region of France and Belgium where it originated over 1,000 years ago. It is believed to have descended from the prehistoric Solutré horse and is one of the oldest draft breeds in France. Used both for war and farm work, the modern Ardennais is heavier and more massive than it was during the 1600s through 1800s. This greater size and strength came from crossing the Ardennais with other draft breeds, such as the Belgian, Percheron and Boulonnais. Despite its bulk, the Ardennais is known for its gentleness.

Conformation:

Large, expressive head with straight profile and blunt muzzle, small ears. Very thick, wide, bulky body. Sloping shoulder. Powerful, deep chest. Short, broad back. Wide, muscular hindquarters. Sturdy legs with some feathering on lower legs. Strong, sound hooves.

Characteristics:

Common colors are roan, bay and chestnut. Known for its hardiness, strength, endurance and pleasant nature.

What can I use it for?
Farm and carriage work.

How tall is it?
15 to 16 hands

Where does it come from?
France and Belgium, Europe

Temperament:
Quite gentle, obedient and easy to handle. Very kind disposition.

Auxois

Background:
An extremely heavy and powerful horse, the Auxois originated in Belgium and is believed to have descended from the Burgundy horse of the Middle Ages. The Auxois is closed related to the Ardennais in appearance, and has been improved through the years by crosses with the Ardennais, Percheron and Boulonnais. Pulling power is the prime trait of the sturdy Auxois and this has made the breed popular for farm work. Known for its tremendous strength and endurance, the hard-working Auxois is kind and easy to handle.

Conformation:
Large, short head with wide forehead and small, pricked ears. Stout, well-muscled neck and prominent withers. Heavy, bulky body. Wide chest. Short, broad back. Powerfully muscled hindquarters. Low-set tail. Stout, strong legs with light feathering.

Characteristics:
Typically bay or roan in color. Known for good gaits, despite its massive size.

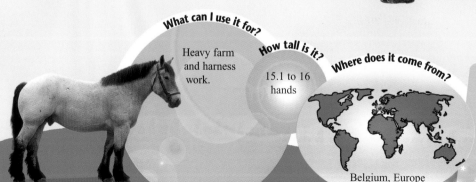

What can I use it for?
Heavy farm and harness work.

How tall is it?
15.1 to 16 hands

Where does it come from?
Belgium, Europe

Temperament:
Quiet and gentle. Even-tempered and a willing worker.

Boulonnais

Background:

Sometimes referred to as the "thoroughbred of draft horses" because of its elegance, the handsome Boulonnais was once used as a war horse in the Middle Ages. Some historians believe the Boulonnais traces back to the days of Julius Caesar's cavalry. The bloodlines of Spanish horses and the Arabian contributed to the breed's stamina and beauty. Known for their speedy trot, Boulonnais were routinely used to transport fresh fish from Boulogne to Paris during the 17th century. Unfortunately, there are far fewer Boulonnais today than in the early 1900s, as the area of France where the horses were bred suffered much damage during World Wars I and II.

Conformation:

Elegant, refined head with flat, broad forehead, large eyes, and small, alert ears. Thick, arched neck with thick, double mane. Well-defined withers. Broad, deep chest. Sloping shoulder. Straight back and compact body. Strong legs with short cannon bones. Slight feathering on lower legs.

Characteristics:

Most are gray. Known for endurance, good gaits and long stride.

What can I use it for?
Farm work, driving and carriage businesses.

How tall is it?
15.3 to 16.3 hands

Where does it come from?
France, Europe

Temperament:
Gentle and easy-going, yet spirited and energetic. Agile, willing worker.

Belgian/Brabant

Background:
During the Middle Ages, this ancient European breed was known as the Horse of Flanders and used as both a war horse and for field work. The Flanders Horse contributed to the development of several other draft breeds, such as the Shire, Clydesdale and Suffolk Punch. Breeders in Belgium used the horse extensively for working the land, and developed the Belgian, also known as the Brabant, into a versatile heavy horse noted for its power. The Belgian was imported to the United States in the 1880s and is a very popular horse for pulling contests.

Conformation:
Attractive, refined head and short, thick neck. Stout, compact, muscular body. Short back. Extremely powerful, wide hindquarters. Strong, short legs with well-developed gaskins. Some feathering on lower legs. Strong hooves.

Characteristics:
Good stride at the walk, at which most work is done.

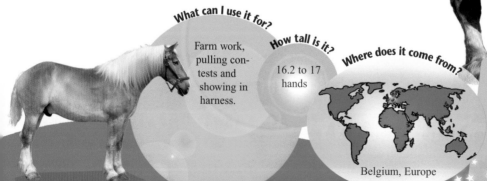

What can I use it for?
Farm work, pulling contests and showing in harness.

How tall is it?
16.2 to 17 hands

Where does it come from?
Belgium, Europe

Temperament:
Quiet, determined, willing worker. Kind disposition.

Breton

Background:

Breeders in France's coastal area of Brittany developed the Breton centuries ago, and the horse was popular during the Middle Ages as a war horse. Crossing with other breeds through the years has resulted in more than one type of Breton. Known for its massive strength, the heavy draft Breton achieved its size through crosses with other draft breeds during the 19th century, including the Ardennais and Percheron. The small Breton draft horse has the same general characteristics of the heavy draft type, but is smaller overall and the face typically has a dished profile. Used for driving and light farm work, the Postier Breton inherited good gaits due to crosses with the Norfolk Trotter and the Hackney during the 19th century. Bretons remain very popular in their native France and are also widely exported to other countries.

Conformation:

Squarish head with wide forehead and typically with a straight profile, although some can have a slightly dished face. Strong, short neck. Long, muscular shoulder. Compact, squarish body. Broad, short, well-muscled back. Wide croup. Short, strong legs with short cannon bones. Light feathering on lower legs.

Characteristics:

Usually chestnut or red roan with flaxen mane and tail. Easy keeper. Good gaits.

What can I use it for?
Farm, harness work and driving.

How tall is it?
15 to 16.2 hands

Where does it come from?
France, Europe

Temperament:
Tractable and pleasant. Willing worker.

Clydesdale

Background:
Developed in the Clyde Valley of Scotland during the early 19th century, the Clydesdale descended from English and Flemish stallions that were crossed on Scottish mares. Known for their high-stepping action and long stride, Clydesdales were used for farm work and hauling loads in the coal fields and cities. By the late 19th century, they were exported to numerous countries, including the United States. Used in the much-publicized Anheuser-Busch hitch, the Clydesdale is a popular draft horse around the world.

Conformation:
Wide forehead and straight profile with high head carriage. Long neck. Powerful body with prominent withers. Long legs with generous white silky feathering on lower leg. Durable, sound, slightly flat hooves.

Characteristics:
Flashy, high knee action and long stride. Considered among the most elegant of the draft breeds. The dominant color is bay, but black, brown, chestnut and roan are also found. White markings on face and legs are common.

What can I use it for?
Farm work, pleasure and show driving, carriage businesses, parades, riding.

How tall is it?
16 to 19 hands

Where does it come from?
Scotland, Europe

Temperament:
Docile, intelligent and willing.

Comtois

Background:
A lightly-built draft horse compared with some other heavy breeds, the Comtois was originally bred in the Franche-Comte and Jura Mountains that border France and Switzerland. Well-suited to working in mountainous regions, this old breed likely descended from horses brought to France in the 4th century by German immigrants. In the 16th century, the Comtois earned regard as a cavalry and artillery horse, and was used by Napoleon in some campaigns. Other draft breeds, including the Percheron and Ardennais, contributed to Comtois bloodlines during the 1800s and 1900s.

Conformation:
Large, attractive head with small ears and alert eyes. Thick, straight, powerful neck. Stocky, compact body. Deep girth. Straight back. Well-muscled hindquarters. Short, sturdy legs. Slight feathering on lower leg.

Characteristics:
Comes in shades of chestnut ranging from reddish to chocolate brown. Mane and tail are flaxen-colored and very thick. Known for their free action, hardiness and longevity.

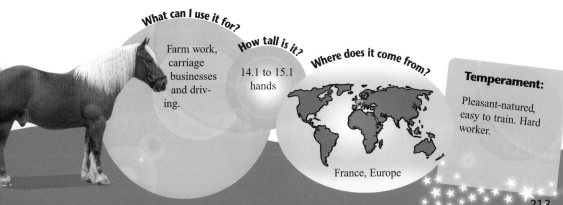

What can I use it for?
Farm work, carriage businesses and driving.

How tall is it?
14.1 to 15.1 hands

Where does it come from?
France, Europe

Temperament:
Pleasant-natured, easy to train. Hard worker.

Dutch Draft

Background:
The heaviest of the Dutch breeds, this massive draft horse was developed in the Netherlands in the early 1900s for heavy farm work and hauling. It bears close resemblance to the Belgian, and indeed, the Dutch Draft Horse was developed by crossing Dutch Zeeland mares with the Belgian and Ardennais. Although large and powerful, the Dutch Draft is known for its kind and quiet temperament. A solid and steady worker, it can also exhibit a lively pace when asked.

Conformation:
Large head with short ears and straight profile.
Short, thick neck. Well-muscled chest.
Stout, compact, muscular body with short back.
Extremely powerful, wide hindquarters. Strong, short legs with well developed gaskins. Feathering on lower leg. Strong hooves.

Characteristics:
Known as a reliable, steady worker for extended periods of time.

What can I use it for?
Farm work, driving and showing in harness.

How tall is it?
16 to 16.3 hands

Where does it come from?
Netherlands, Europe

Temperament:
Very quiet disposition. Dependable and calm. Willing worker.

214

Italian Heavy Draft

Background:
The regions of Northern and central Italy are home to the Italian Heavy Draft, which was developed in the 19th century. Belgian, Breton, Percheron, Boulonnais, Hackney, Arabian and Thoroughbred bloodlines all contributed to the breed's creation. Also known in its native country as "Tiro Pesante Rapido" and "Cavallo da Tiro Rapido," this Italian breed is known for its rapid trot. The mixture of bloodlines in the heritage of the Italian Heavy Draft makes for a powerful and energetic work horse with a long walk and speedy trot.

Conformation:
Long, fine head. Short, crested neck. Powerful shoulder. Broad, deep chest. Compact, deep body. Short, broad, flat back. Strong, rounded hindquarters. High-set tail. Muscular legs with large joints. Some feathering on lower leg.

Characteristics:
Usually liver chestnut with flaxen mane and tail. Easy keeper. Very hardy.

What can I use it for?
Farm and harness work.

How tall is it?
15 to 16 hands

Where does it come from?
Italy, Europe

Temperament:
Gentle and kind, but lively. Willing worker.

Jutland

Background:
Denmark is the home of this medium-sized draft breed that likely descended from horses belonging to the Vikings. Breeds that contributed to the Jutland are the Suffolk Punch, Frederiksborg and possibly the Shire. Named after the Jutland Peninsula where it has been bred for centuries, the Jutland was once a mount for knights going to battle. Known for their stamina and strength, today's Jutlands are used to pull brewery wagons and for other draft work.

Conformation:
Somewhat plain head with squared muzzle. Short, thick neck. Flat withers. Heavily muscled shoulder. Broad chest. Deep girth. Compact, thick, rounded body. Short, sturdy legs. Coarse, heavy feathering on lower leg.

Characteristics:
Usually chestnut with flaxen mane and tail.

What can I use it for?
Draft and carriage work.

How tall is it?
15.2 to 16 hands

Where does it come from?
Denmark, Europe

Temperament:
Gentle and kind. Willing worker.

Murakozi

Background:
Also known as the Hungarian Draft, the Murakozi originated during the late 1800s and early 1900s in the River Mura area of Hungary. The Murakozi was created by crossing native Hungarian mares with several breeds, including the Noriker, Percheron, Ardennes, and Arabian. The resulting horse was perfect for agricultural work such as plowing, but also quick and active. The Murakozi matures at an early age and can be worked as young as two years old.

Conformation:
Large, attractive head often with slightly convex profile. Compact, powerful build. Deep girth. Pronounced dip in back. Rounded, powerfully-muscled hindquarters. Sloping croup. Low-set tail. Strong, short legs. Slight feathering at heel.

Characteristics:
Usually chestnut with flaxen mane and tail. Known to be easy keepers.

What can I use it for?
Farm and harness work, driving.

How tall is it?
15.3 to 16.1 hands

Where does it come from?
Hungary, Europe

Temperament:
Kind and even-tempered. Willing and energetic.

Mulassier/Poitevin

Background:

This French breed of heavy draft horse is known internationally as the Poitou, but in its native country, it is referred to as the Mulassier or Poitevin. The breed was created by crossing local horses with Dutch stock. Originally developed for heavy agricultural use, over-all numbers of the breed have decreased due to the use of mechanization on farms. Today, the breed is considered potentially endangered. It is found mainly in the Pays de Loire and Poitou-Charentes areas of France. The Mulassier/Poitevin is also used to pro-duce large, powerful work mules.

Conformation:

Large heavy head often with convex profile. Thick neck. Broad chest. Deep girth. Strong, short back. Wide, powerful hindquarters. Short, thick legs with broad joints. Abundant feathering on lower legs.

Characteristics:

Equal in pulling power to the Percheron.

What can I use it for?

Heavy farm and har-ness work.

How tall is it?

16.3 to 17.1 hands

Where does it come from?

France, Europe

Temperament:

Docile and laid back.

Norwegian Dølahest

Background:
Although horses have been replaced by tractors for much modern farm work, this Norwegian draft breed is making a come-back for use in forestry operations and on smaller family farms. The Dølahest is known as a willing, hard worker capable of working into its twenties. Its easy-going temperament also makes the Dølahest useful as a general riding horse. The breed has even been featured on a Norwegian Christmas postage stamp.

Conformation:
Straight profile. Thick, strong neck. Stout, short-coupled build. Short, wide back. Powerful hindquarters. Short, strong legs with heavy feathering..

Characteristics:
Sturdy and sure-footed.

What can I use it for?
Farm and forestry work, general riding and mountain trekking.

How tall is it?
13 to 15 hands

Where does it come from?
Norway, Europe

Temperament:
Docile and even-tempered, willing and sociable.

Noriker

Background:
The Noriker, also referred to as the Noric Horse, has been bred in Austria for nearly 2,000 years. One of the oldest European cold-blood breeds, the Noriker has strict standards. The first inspection regulations for stallions were drafted as early as 1703. Today, both stallions and mares are inspected and must pass conformation and performance tests. While strength and agility make the Noriker popular as a work horse, it is also well-suited for riding and driving.

Conformation:
Large head. Thick, crested neck. Good shoulder. Broad body with very deep girth.
Strong hindquarters. Sturdy, strong legs and good hooves. Some feathering on lower legs.

Characteristics:
Very thick mane and tail. Known for its soundness and good temperament.

What can I use it for?
Riding, driving, farm and carriage work.

How tall is it?
16 to 17 hands

Where does it come from?
Austria, Europe

Temperament:
Gentle and willing.

Norman Cob

Background:

Normandy, France has been recognized for many centuries as one of the finest horse breeding areas of the world. It is the home of the Norman Cob, also known as the Normandy Cob. This breed was officially recognized in the early 1900s, but its heritage traces back to Roman times when small native horses were crossed with draft-type pack mares to create a strong work horse. Although robust and stocky, it does not have the large dimensions of a heavy draft horse. Used for light draft and farm work, the energetic Norman Cob is known for its excellent, flowing trot.

Conformation:

Large, attractive head with wide forehead and kind eyes. Thick, powerful neck. Overall compact build. Strong, sloping shoulder. Broad, deep chest. Deep girth. Short, strong back. Sloping croup. Short, well-muscled legs with substantial bone and good joints. Slight feathering at heel. Strong hooves.

Characteristics:

Good, free-moving action.

What can I use it for?
Farm and harness work.

How tall is it?
15.3 to 16.3 hands

Where does it come from?
France, Europe

Temperament:
Even-tempered and docile. Willing and kind.

North Swedish Horse

Background:
Descended from the ancient native Scandinavian horse, the North Swedish Horse developed in Sweden around 1900. A smaller breed of heavy horse, the North Swedish is compact and known for its strength. In its native country, it is commonly used as a work horse in both farming and foresty, and can pull weighty loads. Despite its power, the North Swedish also has a good, springy trot and a long, well-balanced stride. Disease is rarely found in this hardy breed.

Conformation:
Large, squarish head. Thick, crested neck. Well-sloped, strong shoulder. Long, strong back. Short legs with plenty of bone. Some feathering on lower leg. Good hooves.

Characteristics:
Known for its endurance and longevity.

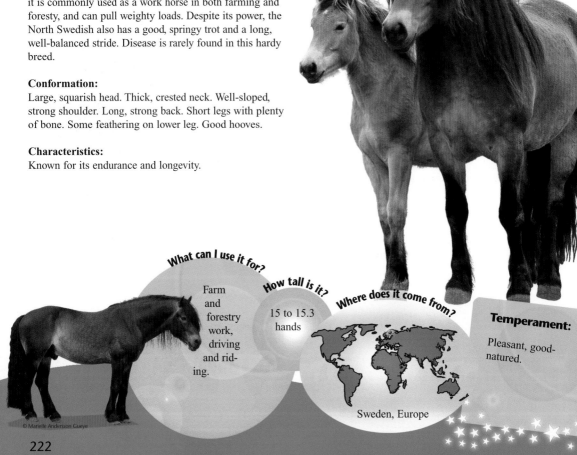

© Marielle Andersson Gueye

What can I use it for?
Farm and forestry work, driving and riding.

How tall is it?
15 to 15.3 hands

Where does it come from?
Sweden, Europe

Temperament:
Pleasant, good-natured.

222

Percheron

Background:
The Percheron is so named because it originated in the Perche region of Normandy, France. Used by knights as war horses as early as AD 732, the breed's early ancestors were more light-bodied than the modern Percheron. Later breeding for agricultural use made the Percheron heavier and more robust. Arabian bloodlines contributed to the Percheron's soundness, beauty and long stride. Jean le Blanc, the most famous Percheron stallion was foaled around 1830, and virtually all of today's Percheron bloodlines trace to him. The breed remains popular for various types of driving and farm work.

Conformation:
Attractive head with straight profile and wide, square forehead. Long, arched neck with plentiful mane. Broad body with short, strong back. Deep chest. Prominent withers. Long shoulder. Strong, short legs. Hard hooves. Very little feathering on lower leg.

Characteristics:
Arabian influence can sometimes be seen in the head. Gray or black are the predominant colors. Known for its free-striding action and style.

© G. Boiselle

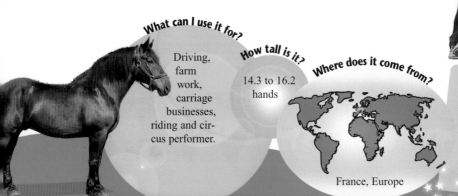

What can I use it for?
Driving, farm work, carriage businesses, riding and circus performer.

How tall is it?
14.3 to 16.2 hands

Where does it come from?
France, Europe

Temperament:
Easy-going, pleasant disposition. Willing, hard worker.

223

Russian Heavy Draft

Background:
This small draft horse breed was established in Russia in the early 1900s and officially recognized in 1952. Russian grade mares were crossed with the Orlov Trotter, Percheron, Belgian and Ardennes to create the Russian Heavy Draft. Known for its great milk-producing capacity and early maturity, the breed is full grown by age three, which is early in comparison to many other draft breeds. The Russian Heavy Draft has short legs for its relatively long body. It is built for pulling and can handle substantial weight.

Conformation:
Clean-cut head with wide forehead and straight profile. Short, broad, well-crested neck. Low withers. Broad, deep chest. Long, broad back. Long, sloping croup. Short, solid legs with front legs set far apart. Some feathering on heel area.

Characteristics:
Reaches physical maturity by age three. Known for its longevity and ability to work well into its 20s.

What can I use it for?
Farm and harness work.

How tall is it?
14.2 to 15.2 hands

Where does it come from?
Russia, Asia

Temperament:
Energetic, but docile. Willing worker.

Shire

Background:

The Great Horse of the Middle Ages was the ancestor of the massive Shire, which is often considered the world's largest horse. Developed in England, the Shire breed was established over 1,000 years ago. The Shire was probably bred as a war horse to carry knights and their heavy armor into battle, and in later centuries was used as a coach horse and for farm work. Their excellent work ethic makes them a popular horse for agricultural work, pulling contests, carriage businesses and showing in harness. For such a large horse, they have flashy action, especially at the trot.

Conformation:

Large head with convex profile, wide forehead and expressive eyes. Long neck. Massive, compact body. Large, deep shoulder. Deep girth. Powerful, rounded hindquarters. Sloping croup. Long, muscular legs. Abundant feathering on lower leg.

Characteristics:

The biggest of the draft breeds, many Shires weigh over 2,000 pounds.
Black with white markings is the most popular color.

What can I use it for?

Driving, farm work, carriage businesses, showing, and pleasure riding.

How tall is it?

17 to 19 hands

Where does it come from?

England, Europe

Temperament:

Strong desire to please. Very gentle.

225

Suffolk Punch

Background:

One of the oldest draft breeds in existence, the Suffolk Punch originated in the Suffolk and Norfolk counties of England. The region's heavy clay soil required a powerful work horse that also had stamina and a docile disposition. Suffolk farmers used their horses for long days in the field and the breed is known for its hard-working abilities. The name Suffolk Punch comes from the horses' uniform, rounded, plump appearance, described by the English as "punched up." The breed's foundation stallion, Crisp's Horse of Ufford, was foaled in 1768. Suffolk Punch horses are known for their longevity and mares are able to produce foals into old age.

Conformation:

Attractive head. Thick, arched neck. Overall rounded, muscular body. Short, strong back. Shorter legs than some draft breeds, with strongly muscled forearms and gaskins. Round, well-sized hooves that wear well, shod or barefoot.

Characteristics:

Great stamina and heart. Always bright chestnut in color, ranging from light gold to dark liver. Some white markings may occur on lower legs and face. Very symmetrical and uniform in both color and body type.

What can I use it for?

Farm work, logging, pleasure driving and carriage businesses.

How tall is it?

16.1 to 17 hands

Where does it come from?

England, Europe

Temperament:

Docile and easygoing. Willing worker.

Vladimir Heavy Draft

Background:

Officially recognized in 1946, the Vladimir Heavy Draft was developed in the Ivanovo and Vladimir regions of Russia. Large native Russian harness mares were crossed with draft stallions, including the Clydesdale, Percheron, Suffolk and Shire. Despite its size and strength, the Vladimir is known for its free moving gaits and good speed. For a draft breed, they can be quite energetic.

Conformation:

Long, clean-cut head with either straight or convex profile. Muscular neck. Broad chest. Rather long, slightly dipped back. Long, moderately-sloped croup. Long, well-set legs. Feathering on lower leg.

Characteristics:

Bay is most common color. Known for its excellent gaits.

What can I use it for?
Draft and harness work.

How tall is it?
16 to 16.3 hands

Where does it come from?
Russia, Asia

Temperament:
Spirited and energetic.

© Marielle Andersson Gueye

North Swedish Horse

Clydesdale

Shire

Clydesdale

231

Percherons

Jutlands

Shire

Conformation

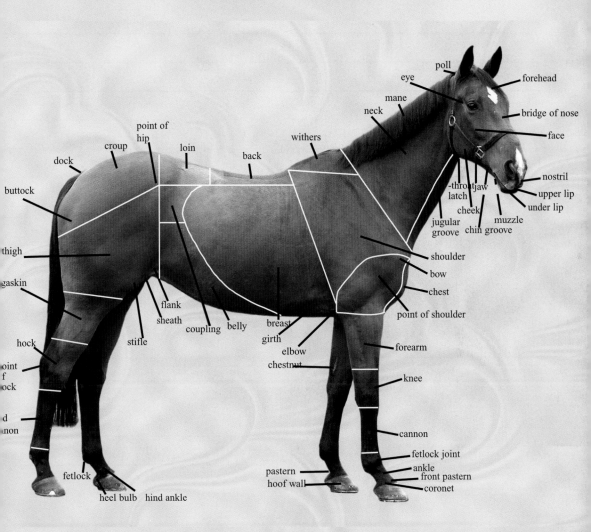

poll

eye

forehead

mane

bridge of nose

neck

face

withers

nostril

upper lip

under lip

throatlatch

jaw

cheek

muzzle

chin groove

jugular groove

point of hip

loin

back

croup

dock

shoulder

bow

buttock

chest

point of shoulder

thigh

forearm

gaskin

hock

flank

sheath

coupling

belly

breast

girth

elbow

chestnut

knee

point of hock

sheath

stifle

cannon

fetlock joint

ankle

front pastern

coronet

pastern

hoof wall

fetlock

heel bulb

hind ankle

Notes

_____   _____

_____   _____

_____   _____

_____   _____

_____   _____

_____

                                    _____

                                    _____

                                    _____

As a full-time freelance writer, Cynthia McFarland writes for a number of national equine publications, including *Horse Illustrated, Thoroughbred Times, Florida Horse, Ocala Style, Texas Thoroughbred, Equine Journal*, and others. She is the author of two non-fiction children's books, *Cows in the Parlor: A Visit to a Dairy Farm* and *Hoofbeats: The Story of a Thoroughbred*. She has recently completed a book on foaling and raising your first foal, which will be published in the fall of 2005.

Cynthia lives on a small farm in the horse country of Ocala, Florida. She has two horses, Ben and Sierra, and loves to spend time trail riding.

Bob Langrish has established a firm reputation as one of the foremost international equestrian photographers. After 30 years in the field, he has built up a complete equestrian photographic library of over 300,000 slides. He has completely illustrated over 100 books, including a number of unique guides compiled in collaboration with various equestrian experts. His photographs are regularly featured in magazines worldwide and his horse calendars are popular with all ages. He has taken photographs at four Olympic Games and works for top equestrian magazines in more than 12 countries around the world. Bob Langrish lives in a beautiful period house in the center of the Regency town of Cheltenham Spa, United Kingdom.

To Ben, my "good little buddy" – thanks for all the great rides.
Here's to many more!
And to Jack – you bring me joy and fill my heart.